Sharon Curtin, who is young, wrote this book in love and anger. In fresh, unaffected prose, clear as water and potent as gin, she tells of her friends among old people and of how our society has treated them.

We dote on youth. We shelve the old. And what does this say about how we view the whole of life?

The author, who grew up in a small town in Wyoming, learned from her grandparents what the rewards of old age can be, and should be. Vigorous, eccentric, loving people, wanted and needed by their clan, they had the time and wisdom to help a child learn and grow. On becoming a registered nurse, Ms. Curtin moved all over the country, seeking out old people as friends and as patients. Her portraits range from a "bag lady," who skulks through New York City carrying all her possessions in two paper bags, to a rich, correct old matron inwardly raging over the lost opportunities that made up her life. Ms. Curtin shared the squalors of a "pensioners' hotel" with two tough old men who taught her panhandling, shoplifting and the other survival skills of the aged poor. Posing as her daughter, she accompanied a spirited old lady on inspections of various vanilla-bland "retirement villages." She tended a brilliant mathematician in the mindless anomie of a nursing home. She fought the social-work bureaucracy for the sake of a sick old man and his insane wife in a state mental hospital. As a Visiting Nurse, she saw a plucky old man caring, with tenderness, skill and respect,

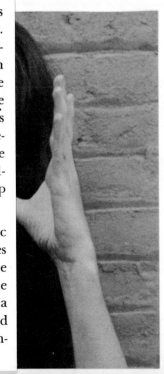

Nobody
Ever Died
of
Old Age

Nobody
Ever Died
of
Old Age

Sharon R. Curtin

An Atlantic Monthly Press Book

LITTLE, BROWN AND COMPANY · BOSTON · TORONTO

FIRST EDITION

T 01/73

Library of Congress Cataloging in Publication Data

Curtin, Sharon R
    Nobody ever died of old age.

    "An Atlantic Monthly Press book."
    1. Aged--United States. 2. Aging. 3. Old
age homes--United States. I. Title.
HV1461.C87   362.6'0973   72-6157
ISBN 0-316-16546-8

ATLANTIC–LITTLE, BROWN BOOKS
ARE PUBLISHED BY
LITTLE, BROWN AND COMPANY
IN ASSOCIATION WITH
THE ATLANTIC MONTHLY PRESS

Published simultaneously in Canada
by Little, Brown & Company (Canada) Limited

PRINTED IN THE UNITED STATES OF AMERICA

To Jim Gordon

Nobody
Ever Died
of
Old Age

One

MY Grandfather Curtin used to refer to old age as "a hell of a long sentence, with no time off for good behavior." It was his habit to wander in and out of rooms and in and out of conversations, providing what his wife Carrie regarded as a perpetually disruptive presence. Almost every little witticism would be followed by a shocked, "Oh, Willy!" as Willy would tell hilariously involved stories of his days as a railroad man, a homesteader, a boxer, an auctioneer; of the time he came back from town and drove the team into the cyclone cellar thinking it was the barn; of his courting days when Carrie's parents referred to him as "that rake"; and of all the chances he

3

had to make money but never did, "because the Irish are lucky in love and unlucky with money." When he died, Carrie and Willy had been married better than sixty-five years. They had seldom been separated. Once, Willy had to go to Oklahoma to have cataracts removed from his eyes (in the process he took a side trip to Texas because, as he explained to a frantic family and the police, he had never been there). And sometimes during the bad years on the farm he would take a job to pull them through.

He would tell us stories, and Carrie would tell him to remember to go to confession on Saturday for being such an outrageous liar. Every morning Carrie would go to Mass to pray for Willy's soul; every afternoon he would go down to the local pool hall to sit and smoke his pipe and swap lies with the other old men.

Willy used to tell the story of how, when they first came to Wyoming to homestead, the wagon broke down a few miles from the shack. It was a day in early spring when the last of the winter winds throws each bit of snow with skin-piercing rancor and a clear blue sky sends the mocking promise of an early thaw. The young Curtin family had to walk the last few miles to their new home. In the process, Willy fell through the ice in a bordering creek. He was carrying a suitcase and the infant Paul, and as he tells it, he "dropped Paul in the freezing crick and saved the suitcase, because the Irish always have another baby but I had only one good suit."

Once, when I was home with my first car — a sports car — Willy decided to take it for a drive. By this time he was almost totally blind (the cataract operations were successful, but he insisted on wearing glasses from the local five-and-ten instead of the special lenses, so he never recovered his vision) and couldn't hear too well, either. But he was very proud of having the first Wyoming driver's license and renewed it regularly. He knew the way to the pool hall by instinct; unfortunately, a lumber truck stopped rather suddenly and he was surprised by the intrusion of several pine boards through the windshield. That crazy old man, I remember thinking. Doesn't he know he's old? He should be locked up. Carrie went to Mass to pray for her husband the car thief.

Willy and Carrie. When I was very young, they still had a small farm and we spent some time there, especially the times when my mother was having another baby. Carrie would refer to it as a "blessed event, a little gift from God," and Willy would take us out to the barn to see a litter of kittens being born.

The atmosphere in the house was one of sin about to be committed. Deeply religious, Carrie was always on the watch for the fallen. And regularly one of us would fall from grace. Eating between meals was a sin; the cookie jar was always full. Fighting was a sin; we were a large family of radically different opinions, and voices were constantly raised to cover the sound of fists pounding the table. Disrespect for the cloth was a super-sin; the local priest was a poker buddy of Willy's and would slip to the cellar for a between-games sip. When I was ten, and decided to become the first female atheist in the Curtin family, refusing to attend Mass and catechism class, I soon felt as if the full weight of Saint Patrick's holy staff had been brought upon me by Carrie Cecilia Keenan Curtin. She threatened me with everything from eternal damnation to being responsible for her own death from shame; and when nothing else worked, decided to ignore me forever. Willy tried to explain that, as generations of nonbelievers before me, I should honor my grandmother by attending Mass. He had done so ever since their marriage. "If there is a God, it can't hurt to have him on our side," he explained. Willy was a man who lived comfortably with contra-dictions.

Carrie really was a saint. All Irish grandmothers are saints, I suspect. She would giggle like a girl when Willy would tease about their courting days and flee the room whenever he would get a bit ribald. Carrie had a lot of suitors, Willy would say; she had

6

been a schoolteacher and every lazy scallawag in Nebraska wanted her to support them. And Carrie would call out from the next room that she only married him to save his soul from the devil. I think the family myth was that Carrie would save us all in the end; certainly she put a match to enough candles to blacken the ceiling of any church.

I remember my mother's father, called Granddad, as a small silent man, a cabinetmaker and carpenter with a liking for strong drink. For a time I guess he was the town drunk, and my memories of him are as fogged by shame as his mind was by whiskey. When he was working — and he managed to support himself until his death — he was a different man. I remember watching him build a cabinet in our house; his hands were craftsman's hands, marked by his trade. The ends of two fingers were missing, lost in the first power saw brought to the county, when they built a bridge over the North Platte. The nails of the remaining fingers were ridged, horny, discolored, misshapen, not like fingernails but more like the claws of some very old and tough bird. The knuckles had been crushed and mauled until each had its own special shape and size. Every inch of skin was mapped by the building he had done. I can't remember his face and can't forget those hands. When he touched wood those mutilated old hands would turn into something beautiful, as if pure love was flowing from his fingers into the wood.

When Granddad was about sixty-five years old, the doctors told him he would die of cirrhosis within a year if he didn't stop drinking. He kept building houses and remodeling kitchens, and he also kept drinking. When he was seventy, he had a heart attack, and the doctors said, Fred, this time it is certain death. No alcohol, rest, quit working. Again he lived as he always had. Work hard, drink hard. When he was seventy-four, he developed a huge growth in his abdomen and exploratory surgery revealed massive cancer. Ah, Fred, said the doctors. This is it. Six months, a year maybe. Eight years later, walking down the road to do some work on a barn, a bit unsteady on his feet from a night on the town, he was hit by a truck and killed. I don't think he ever listened to another human being, not even doctors. He knew the communication between hands and tools and wood, but none of the human tongues.

During the last twenty years of his life there were many attempts to put Granddad in the local old folks home. In most small towns there is a place for the senile, the infirm, the unwanted; a place for impecunious old loners to die in obscurity. Most families took care of their own; only those without relatives were residents. Occasionally someone had "family" inside and this was treated as a secret shame. "Poor old Fred," said the town gossips, "he just couldn't take it anymore. He's up at the old folks home." Heads would shake and old Fred would be forgotten.

This old folks home was called the Old Doyle Place after the man who had built it. He had been a rancher and a banker and believed that Douglas, Wyoming, was going to be the next Chicago. (The railroad went through Douglas, as had the Oregon trail. But all the local growth and industry went to Casper, fifty miles west.) The style was Prairie Gothic, with towers and gingerbread trim and wide porches. All the windows seemed to be in the wrong places; it was a house designed to hold the darkness. After Doyle's fortune disappeared the house was sometimes a rooming house and sometimes deserted. Finally an enterprising local widow began to take in people who lived "on the county," and Doyle's proud dream house became the "Old Folks Home."

I remember visiting that place once or twice. (I have no clear memory of why; I don't remember seeing Granddad there.) I thought the house was haunted. It seemed full of stairs and shadows. Some of the shadows moved and swayed; old people rocking the years back and forth. The air was full of the smells of every human function — I could almost see bits of shit and vomit and piss and sweat floating around — and the woman showing me around kept a handkerchief to her nose. We went up the stairs and she introduced me to some of the old people. I remember one old man gave me candy; on the floor by his bed was an old tin can he used as a spittoon. "Teebee. Coughing my life away," he told me. He didn't seem sad or angry, just patient. The old women on the next floor fluttered around me, their hands reaching out to touch and tug and pull and exclaim over my hair, my freckles, my blue eyes. Their touch had no substance, like a dry wind on a July afternoon. When I ran down the stairs, I could hear their voices begging: "Come back soon, come back and see us, we'll have a party, come back soon . . ."

I did go back a few times. Someone taught me to embroider, another gave me her secret recipe for nut bread (which I promptly lost), old men told me tales of Indian raids and cattle wars, and hard times, until my eyes grew so round they matched my open mouth. After a while I stopped coming. And on Halloween I would join the other kids running up to pound on the door of the "haunted house" to prove my bravery, ashamed to admit I had been inside and found nothing so fearsome about the old men and women who lived there.

Granny had left her husband and five children years before. When I was growing up, my father would mention to my mother that her mother had deserted her. (I always thought it a terribly brave and romantic thing for Granny to have done; and that was before I read *A Doll's House* or *The Golden Notebook* or heard of women's liberation.) My earliest memories of Granny have to do with her size. She was about four feet, nine inches tall, just the right size for a fairy godmother. And since we only saw her during summer vacation, and since her past was shrouded by adult whispers, I always thought she *was* my fairy godmother. She was a storyteller too, and would talk about being a woman on her own during the Depression years, or working in a restaurant for senators in Washington that "only hired red-haired waitresses," of hitchhiking across the country to San Diego; of surviving without education or skills. This grandmother was a swinger by any standards. When I visited her apartment in San Diego — she was in her seventies — the foyer was dominated by a huge poster of Elvis Presley.

When Granny came back to Wyoming to visit her children, she would bring her "friend" Emery. I adored him — he looked just like Jimmy Durante — and I named a kitten after him. I think her grown children were scandalized by their mother's behavior. I know I wasn't supposed to ask many questions about Emery.

Shortly after Emery died, Granny (at this time she was about seventy-five) got a new "friend" and decided she wanted to get married again. But her children, adults with married children and grandchildren of their own, were solidly against the marriage. Granny was never one to argue with closed minds, so she eloped with the man who everyone felt was too young for her and probably after her money. He was over sixty and Granny had her social security check and maybe a little money saved.

I like to think of her, seventy-eight years old, climbing down a ladder to run away with the "smooth-talking stranger."

Granny and her "friend" (no one is sure if they ever really got married) moved to North Carolina, where, at the age of eighty-three, she was running to catch a bus and was hit by a truck. Death was instantaneous, the telegram said, and she didn't know what hit her. I think Granny always knew exactly what was hitting her, and probably took the license number of the truck as she died; I am also sure she was aware of the irony of dying in the same manner as her long-ago deserted husband. Her children shifted his coffin over a bit and buried her at Fred's side. She would have seen the irony in that, too.

Only Carrie is left, and like all Irish saints she has been saying for years she is ready to go, and it would be a blessing and a joy to join the Lord. At ninety-six, she'll outlast us all, lighting candles at every wake.

Two

THOSE were my grandparents. Three lived full, independent lives until they died suddenly, and Carrie is still lighting the family's way to heaven with votive candles. Their aging process seemed as natural as my own; as I gained a little and lost a little, so did they. I was aware of the times they stumbled or misunderstood what people said, but I was pretty clumsy and didn't always listen either. Carrie's hair turned pure white, and Willy lost all his. On the other hand, Granny was a redhead until her death. (Probably still, in her coffin, has that defiant red flag flying.)

Once Willy set fire to the house by absentmindedly knocking out a warm pipe into the clothes hamper. And Carrie had a bad fall soon after, breaking her hip and raising the question of whether she would walk again. There was called that solemn family meeting to discuss What To Do With The Old Folks.

That's when I began to understand growing old wasn't natural.

Like conspirators the old walk all bent over, as if hiding some precious secret, filled with self-protection. The body seems to gather itself around those vital parts, folding shoulders, arms, pelvis like a fading rose. Watch and you see how fragile old people come to think they are made.

Aging paints every action gray, lies heavy on every movement, imprisons every thought. It governs each decision with a ruthless and single-minded perversity. To age is to learn the feeling of no longer growing, of struggling to do old tasks, to remember familiar actions. The cells of the brain are destroyed with thousands of unfelt tiny strokes, little pockets of clotted blood wiping out memories and abilities without warning. The body seems to slowly give up, randomly stopping, starting again as if to torture and tease with the memory of lost strength. Hands become clumsy, frail transparencies, held together with knotted blue veins, fluttering in front of your eyes and reminding you of growing infirmity.

Sometimes it seems as if the distance between your feet and the floor is constantly changing, as if you walk on shifting and not quite solid ground. One foot down, slowly, carefully, force the other foot forward. Sometimes you are a shuffler, not daring to lift your feet from the uncertain earth but forced to slide hesitantly forward in little whispering movements. Sometimes you are able to really "step out" but this effort — in fact the pure exhilaration of easy movement — soon exhausts you.

The world becomes narrower as friends and family die or move away. To climb stairs, to ride in a car, to walk to the corner, to talk on the telephone; each action seems to take energy needed to stay alive. Everything is limited by the strength you hoard greedily. Your needs decrease, you require less food, less sleep, and finally less human contact; yet this little bit becomes more and more difficult. You fear that one day you will be reduced to the simple acts of breathing and taking nourishment. This is the ultimate stage you dread, the period of helplessness and hopelessness, when any further independence will be over.

There is nothing to prepare you for the experience of growing old. Living is a process, an irreversible progression toward old age and eventual death. You see men of eighty still vital and tall and straight as oaks; you see men of fifty reduced to gray shadows in the human landscapes. The cellular clock differs for each one of us, and is profoundly affected by our own life experiences, our heredity, and perhaps most importantly, by the concepts of aging encountered in society and in oneself.

Nobody ever died of old age.

Accidents kill, cancer kills, bullets kill, coronary occlusions kill; but no one ever died just because of age. Today in the United States there are twenty million persons over sixty-five. Modern medicine has enabled man to survive the diseases of early and middle age and live to a "ripe old age" hitherto unknown except in Biblical lore. Most families have members who are in their late eighties. Hearts beating to a rhythm set by quinidine and digitalis, they are kept free of the killer pneumonia by antibiotics, kept walking with cortisone and aspirin for crippling arthritis. We see grandmothers who are glamour queens on stage and screen, and men who continue to be masculine idols in their seventies. With increasing frequency we read in the newspapers the advice of another man or woman who has celebrated a century of life: Don't drink, don't swear, don't fornicate. (There are presently fifteen thousand Americans over 100 years of age and each receives a birthday card from the President of the United States.) But living forever is no longer a moral victory; it is a miracle of modern chemistry. The process of aging has become a medical specialty.

We treat as diseases two natural processes: birth and aging; the beginning and the end of life. For most Americans — indeed for most members of Western societies — life begins and ends in a hospital, attended by specialists. The doctor is the usher, taking us up and down the aisles, robbing us all of privacy, intimacy, dignity; and substituting "sterility," "science," "objectivity." The family unity, the community, the single individual is cheated, robbed, demeaned by this ushering in and out of life, down a clean, white and emotionless corridor.

We need to understand a good deal more about these natural processes, and remove the professional cloak of myth and mystery that surrounds the processes of life and of death.

From a biological point of view, aging is simply a process of change, a continuous development which takes place in a fairly regular manner throughout our lives. In each individual that pace may differ. (This depends on factors as divergent as age of parents at the time of our birth — offspring of young parents tend to live longer — and general physical health throughout life.) Different parts of the body resist aging more than others, and abilities fade at different rates.

One of the major factors of the aging process is a gradual and unpredictable breakdown of the body's reaction to stress. Throughout our lives, we are subject to life-threatening forces — invasion by bacteria, infiltration by viruses, trauma incurred in falls, fat in our arteries, and so on — so that our physical being seems to be under constant siege. This state of siege is met by a complex and wonderful protective mechanism designed to prolong life and maintain physical integrity. In time, even with the best of care and the most protective environment, this defense system becomes less efficient and itself is under attack by the aging process.

Three glands, the pituitary (tucked under the brain) and the adrenals (on either side of the kidneys) secrete hormones which vitally influence the resistance of the body to stress. They govern the body's response to attack. If you cut yourself, hormones cause an immediate response: they hasten the clotting of blood, lower blood pressure to control the rate of bleeding, increase blood sugar levels to provide more energy. If you are subjected to cold, hormones constrict arteries, raise the blood pressure, and cause you to shiver to provide warmth. If you develop an infection, hormones cause the body to increase blood supply in the area and produce the mechanisms, such as inflammation, with which we fight an invasion of bacteria. The hormones can be seen as the message units which marshal all our strength and resources to protect an endangered body.

When this protective system breaks down, or is interfered with, which happens when an individual ages and when he is under increasing stress, the body is subject to debilitating and degenerative diseases as well as less resistant to acute illness. Arthritis, arteriosclerosis, hypertension, are all indications that the defense mechanism is functioning less efficiently. As one grows older, the reserve capacity to withstand physical stress becomes less and less. It is as if the failsafe mechanism no longer functions. The doctor may say the cause of illness is pneumonia caused by one sort of bacteria or another, but the body knows that the failure exists within. The hormones could not gather the forces to fight the infection.

This means that an influenza epidemic, which is simply inconvenient and uncomfortable for most people, kills thousands of the aged. As we age, small things become killers. Our resources of resistance decrease and there is an increase in the chances we will be called upon to respond to stress greater than the body can stand. An example of this kind of threat is the foulness of the air city dwellers are forced to breathe: A young person, with healthy, efficient lungs will survive, but an old person may find it contributes to a rather earlier death than necessary.

Another example: chronic hearing loss in the aged. Sixty-five percent of all those affected with gradual loss of hearing are over sixty-five. This percentage is increasing. So is noise pollution. And it is the aged who are least able to withstand the effects of the damage caused by living in an increasingly noisy society. By the time the next generation buys their first cane, they had better know how to lip-read, because they will have been subjected to damaging noise levels throughout their lives. The irony lies in the fact that man invents better and more cosmetic hearing aids, but does little to lower the noise level.

Everyone knows their physical appearance will change as they grow older. It can be emotionally unsettling, even depressing, to look in the mirror and see the effects of the normal aging process. It's not just vanity that makes people hate growing old; the sheer inevitability of the process is frightening, even terrifying. Every aspect of human life undergoes some change as the years march on; the structures and functions of the body gradually become impaired; motivation, perception, emotions alter; the person's position in society and adjustment to surroundings and other people are affected. Some people suffer severe mental torture at the sign of the first gray hair or run to the plastic surgeon for the repair of the first wrinkle. Others seem barely aware of the changes; others simply accept aging as part of the life process. The emotional response to aging is as varied from individual to individual as the process itself. The fact remains that we spend about one quarter of our life growing up and three quarters growing old.

Certain biological changes which occur as we grow older are apparent whenever you look at an old person. The hair becomes thin, brittle, dull, and gray. The skin becomes paler and may become blotchy; it takes on a parchmentlike texture and loses its elasticity. The loss of subcutaneous fat and elastic tissue leads to a wrinkled appearance. Sweat gland activity and oil secretion decrease and the skin may look dry and scaly. These age changes in the surface of the body are gradual, and vary according to diet, genetic factors, even climate. Like all other aspects of aging, it is not the biological changes themselves (because they are, after all, quite natural) but the subsequent changes in self-regard which have the most impact on the individual. Gray hair can be softening and becoming to a woman; and look quite distinguished on a man. Yet the individual may resent the change, and regard gray hair as the external sign of all the internal effects — slowness, muscular weakness, waning sexual powers.

The individual may appear to shrink with age. Full stature is reached in the late teens; afterwards there is little or no change in the length of the bones. There may be a slight loss in overall height due to atrophy of the discs between the vertebrae, and this may be exaggerated by a stooping posture due to muscular weakness. As age advances, the bones become brittle and this increases the risk of breakage. Movements of the joints become stiffer and more restricted as the cartilage between the joints wears thin and the fluid that lubricates their inner surface decreases. After the age of twenty-five or thirty there is a gradual and small reduction in the power and efficiency of muscular contractions, and the ability to sustain effort decreases. This is due to an increase of fibrous material in the muscle tissue and a loss of elasticity. Again, there are vast individual differences, and exercise can improve muscles that have fallen into disuse. After the age of fifty the number of active muscle fibers steadily decreases, and the aged person may appear "wasted" or "all skin and bones."

The body requires food to produce energy, to develop and renew its tissues, and to maintain temperature. People vary in the exact proportions of proteins, carbohydrates, fats, minerals, vitamins, and water required to maintain health, but this difference is more a function of what sort of life is led — the amount of activity, the climate, the state of general health, physical size — than of age. On the whole, the digestive system is less impaired by aging than some other systems, yet older people complain more about digestive functions. Deficiencies of diet are frequently responsible for illness in old age. The older person says he has no appetite, or may live alone and neglect himself. Food doesn't taste the same as the senses of taste and smell become slightly less acute, the taste buds decrease in number and sensitivity, and the mucous membrane lining of the nose thins. Older people secrete less saliva and enzymes necessary for the breakdown of food prior to entry in the stomach. All of this, coupled with conservative food preferences and low budgets, may make it difficult to ensure an adequate diet. There is such a close relationship between eating habits and emotional states that depressed, upset, old people have been known to starve themselves to death.

Most people over sixty-five wear glasses, as the lens of the eye becomes more opaque and less elastic. The lens becomes less able to change focus and the pupil of the eye becomes slower in its reaction time to light. The iris fades and the cornea thickens and becomes less transparent; this is why an aged person's eyes appear almost cloudy in color. There is also a gradual loss of the fatty tissue supporting the eye, so that eventually the eye appears shrunken and the eyelids hang loosely because of poor muscle tone.

Loss of hearing in adults is gradual and may not be noticed because most of the sounds which are relevant to his behavior remain audible. The ability to hear high-pitched sounds is usually lost. There is some degeneration of the auditory nerve. Hearing loss is greater among men, probably because of prolonged excessive noise on the job.

The general effect of aging is to reduce respiratory efficiency; the lungs contain a smaller volume of air, and are less able to expel residual air. Poor oxygenation, though only one factor of biological aging, may be crucial in that adverse changes in the respiratory system can cause temporary impairment of nervous functions.

In general, replacement of elastic, functional tissue by inelastic fibrous cells is both frequent and widespread. If there is any process of "simple aging," distinct from ordinary disease, it is this change in the cells of the different physical systems which make up the organism called man.

The normal, natural process of aging can perhaps

best be regarded as an accumulation of functional losses to which the average person tries to accommodate in some socially acceptable fashion. Diseases of the heart and blood vessels, digestive disorders, arthritis, cancer, impairment of vision and hearing; all are common among the aged. In fact, physical discomfort and even painful illnesses are so often regarded as "normal" for the aged person that they frequently fail to consult a doctor.

Old Jim Crowe was one of those who regarded the aches and pains of his sixty-nine-year-old body as just another dividend from a punishing Scotch-Presbyterian deity. He rented a tiny room from a large family who badly needed the extra money but begrudged him the space he occupied in "their" home. He had no family, had never married, and most of his social contacts came from his daily visits to sit in the sun on the porch of a nearby parsonage. I used to tease Mrs. McCarthy, who kept house for the minister, about her loyal and steady admirer. During the spring and summer, regular as the sun, you would see him nosing his way down the block, stopping every few steps as if to catch a special smell, standing long on the corners before stepping off into the street. He was the only man I have ever known who wore a derby hat. I think the hat was very old, because it was a little large, resting on the tips of his ears and flattening them forward like those of a curious hound. Old Jim was very bald; perhaps the hat was bought when he had the hair to hold it at the proper rakish angle. He wasn't quaint or queer; he held himself too proudly for one to pity him. He was distant and proper. For example, he always tipped his hat to me once I started high school. And I always had an urge to curtsy back.

It seems to me that Old Jim Crowe tried very hard to occupy as little space as possible. He never gestured when he spoke, and spoke as little as anyone I've ever known. He never bored anyone with long stories, like most of the other old men in town, and he never caused a ripple of interest either. He was a fixture, like the WPA mural on the post office wall; no one ever really noticed it until someone covered it with paint.

That is what happened with Old Jim Crowe. I had gone away to nursing school and seldom came home. But one summer I spent a month in Douglas, walking around town, talking to old friends, trying to decide whether or not to continue my education. One morning I stopped to say hello to Mrs. McCarthy and felt a vague discomfort, a sense of something out of place, and I asked her if they had painted recently. It was nothing new that disturbed my eye, but something was missing — Old Jim was not sitting in that tight bundle on the porch swing. The porch was empty.

Mrs. McCarthy told me he was in the local hospital. "He looked so well, so neat, not sloppy like a sick old man. But one day he just keeled over in the swing. Didn't say anything but 'I'm so sorry' over and over again. When I tried to move him, loosen his tie or something, he pushed my hands away. But he was just a bundle of sticks, just a bundle of sticks. I saw him every nice day and never knew he was sick."

I would like to say that Mrs. McCarthy and myself and maybe a few other townspeople missed Old Jim Crowe, but he had been so unassuming and undemanding that the loss felt was also vague and nebulous. People found it hard to believe he was ill because they found it hard to think of him as a physical being at all. He was just a part of the pastor's porch, or a figure in a silly derby hat under the cottonwood trees.

Since, at the time, I was still debating my return to school, I was spending some afternoons in the town hospital. I decided to drop in to see Old Jim Crowe. The nurse on duty told me that he had suffered a mild heart attack, complicated by malnutrition and what she referred to as "his own kind of stubbornness."

What happened is that Old Jim Crowe reached old age with a reasonably good heart. There had been no acute, sudden symptoms to send him running to the doctor. For some months he had felt "indigestion" and some pressure in his chest. But he was an old man, and didn't expect to feel good all the time. Sometimes he felt faint or short of breath . . . but he was an old man . . . or some chest pain, spreading to his arm and back . . . but he was an old man. That day on the porch, he had felt the pain begin to build in his chest. He wanted to get up and walk home to rest, but when he tried to move, the pain increased. He became dizzy and blacked out.

When I first saw him, it was obvious that the most painful thing for him was the embarrassment of being in bedclothes with women around, and the feeling that he had imposed upon Mrs. McCarthy by becoming ill on her porch.

Old Jim Crowe's modesty and humility became a crippling thing. The doctor felt his "attack" had been mild; more in the nature of a warning than a death-blow. With rest, reasonable exercise, good food, relief from any worry, his heart would probably keep pumping away without any sign of permanent damage. One of the things emphasized was the importance of a good diet, preferably small frequent meals, and a quiet, relaxed environment.

But even with all the jovial, well-meaning encouragement the doctor could offer, Old Jim Crowe seemed to regard the diagnosis of heart trouble as a sign on the road to death at best — or at worst, to his becoming a helpless, hopeless invalid. He seemed bent on literally frightening himself to death. Every little twinge would empty his face of color and he would prepare to meet his judge. He was afraid to move, and would lie in bed as stiffly as he once sat in the porch swing. On the other hand, he refused to allow the nurses to perform the simplest tasks for him, preferring to hold his urine until, terrified, he could sneak out of bed rather than have a woman handle the urinal.

The quiet old man began to develop a high fever, chills, and was in obvious pain. He insisted on keeping a urinal in bed with him, although he told his doctor confidentially that he had trouble peeing even though he felt like he had to all the time. Cystitis (an inflammation of the urinary bladder) was diagnosed. In Old Jim's case, the modesty which forced him to retain his urine triggered another physical disability. The urinary tract infection kept Old Jim Crowe bedridden longer than the doctor wanted, but bed rest, antibiotics, and drugs to relieve the pain were all indicated. The heart itself seemed to be doing well, pumping away as if oblivious to the deterioration of the old man's body. There was, at any rate, no indication of organic heart damage.

Once his fever went down, Old Jim Crowe was encouraged to get up and move around. I saw him in the corridor one day. He was walking with his head down; not even walking really, but just doing a half-hearted shuffle. Sometimes he would stop, lean against the wall, and rub the top of his bald head. His ears were still bent forward and made me want to weep for the missing derby. He passed by with his head still down, full of such fatigue and weariness that I could feel the weight on my own shoulders.

I talked to the nurse on duty; she said there was nothing really wrong with him now, but that he needed time to get on his feet. Also the family he had been living with were hesitant to let him move back in until he could promise not to have any more attacks. His obvious loss of vigor and pride was due, said the nurse, ". . . to worry. All he does is worry about this little pain, that little pain. He is so afraid of indigestion, he won't eat right. We have to make him get out of bed. The man just seems to want to stay in the hospital."

Old Jim Crowe, without his derby, without the little bit of space he occupied on the porch, without the strength to bear his ill health. Three days later Mrs. McCarthy told me that Old Jim Crowe had developed some trouble with his leg. The veins in one leg had become inflamed and blocked with blood clots. Diagnosis: thrombophlebitis. Back on bed rest, more medication, more dependence, more chinks in the armor. Every new illness, every new fight back to health, left him with less ability to withstand new attacks.

I went back to school. It wasn't until years later, passing the parsonage and stopping with a vague sense of something missing, something not quite right, that I asked my father, "What ever happened to Old Jim Crowe?"

Three

OLD Jim Crowe becomes more important to me as time goes on. As a matter of fact, he is fairly typical of old people in the United States. The President's Council on Aging, in 1963, drew a "profile" of a citizen over sixty-five:

He is probably not working, and without adequate income.

He is without a high school education.

He receives social security, but no private pension.

He spends most of his income on housing.

When I think of Old Jim Crowe, I realize what that means in human terms, in terms of the way old people have to live. The aged live with enforced leisure, on fixed incomes, subject to many chronic illnesses, and most of their money goes to keep a roof over their heads. But that profile leaves one thing out — Old Jim Crowe had his life-span increased in a culture which worships youth. I don't know which problem to attack first: economics or attitudes.

Attitudes. That used to be what my teachers told me I had plenty of. All wrong. But the kind of culturally, socially enforced attitude I want to talk about makes me bigoted against old people; it makes me think young is best; it makes me treat old people like outcasts.

Hate that gray? Wash it away!
Wrinkle cream.
Monkey glands.
Face lifting.
Look like a bride again.
Old is ugly.
Don't trust anyone over thirty.
I fear growing old.
Feel Young Again!
Old is ugly.

I am afraid to grow old — we're all afraid. In fact, the fear of growing old is so great that every aged person is an insult and a threat to the society. They remind us of our own death — that our body won't

always remain smooth and responsive, but will someday betray us by aging, wrinkling, faltering, failing.
The ideal way to age would be to grow slowly invisible, gradually disappearing, without causing worry
or discomfort to the young. In some ways that does
happen. Sitting in a small park across from a nursing
home one day, I noticed that the young mothers and
their children gathered on one side, and the old
people from the home on the other. Whenever a
youngster would run over to the "wrong" side, chasing a ball or just trying to cover all the available
space, the old people would lean forward and smile.
But before any communication could be established,
the mother would come over, murmuring embarrassed apologies, and take her child back to the
"young" side.

Now, it seemed to me that the children didn't feel
any particular fear, and the old people didn't seem to
be threatened by the children. The division of space
was drawn by the mothers. And the mothers never
looked at the old people who lined the old side of the
park like so many pigeons perched on the benches.
These well-dressed young matrons had a way of *sliding* their eyes over, around, through, the old people;
they never looked at them directly. The old people
might as well have been invisible; they had no reality
for the youngsters, who were not permitted to speak

to them, and they offended the aesthetic eye of the mothers.

My early experiences were somewhat different; since I grew up in a small town, my childhood had more of a nineteenth-century flavor. I knew a lot of old people, and considered some of them friends. There was no culturally defined way for me to "relate" to old people, except the rules of courtesy which applied to all adults. My grandparents were an integral and important part of the family and of the community. I sometimes have a dreadful fear that mine will be the last generation to know old people as friends, to have a sense of what growing old means, to respect and understand man's mortality and his courage in the face of death. Mine may be the last generation to have a sense of living history, of stories passed from generation to generation, of identity established by family history.

It is such an unholy waste. Such a goddamn unholy waste.

Another old man I remember from my childhood was called the "Garbage Man" because he used to scavenge through all the garbage cans in town looking for scraps for his chickens. He was a mother's nightmare of a dirty old man; dressed in tattered stained clothing, an old stocking cap pulled over his head, he shuffled through the alleys of the town pulling a gunny sack. One of his legs was crippled and he wore some sort of heavy shoe, so his step had a special sound. You could hear him coming down the block, step and clump and slide, step and clump! and slide, as he pulled his burdens down the graveled alleys of the town.

Children and dogs teased him. We had a strange mongrel called "Waggles" who would attack anything that was crippled (my mother said he was like a lot of people; he couldn't bear imperfection or any sign of weakness) and someone would always have to hold the dog until the Garbage Man had passed. There was some kind of jingle we used to sing about him:

> *Garbage man, garbage man*
> *Drinks his piss from an old tin can.*
> *Had a wife, away she ran*
> *When she smelled the*
> *Garbage man, garbage man . . .*

The summer I was eight was a drought year. I remember the leaves of the cottonwood trees were dull with dust and the young trees died. They closed the town swimming pool because of a polio scare; so we all swam in the river. That year I developed a consuming curiosity about the Garbage Man. At first I

just became aware I had no idea what his face looked
like. I knew him by his step, and by the jingle that
accompanied him down the alleys, but I had never
seen his face. I knew he was pretty old because my
father said he had been collecting garbage ever since
he could remember. The Garbage Man collected garbage, fed it to his chickens, and sold the eggs back to
the people who provided the garbage.

We weren't allowed to swim in the river, and my
sister told my mother that I had, which resulted in
the hiding of my bathing suit and my restriction to
the yard. So I didn't have much else to do but sit and
stare at the cottonwood trees and wonder about the
Garbage Man.

I developed an elaborate plan of action. I decided
to follow him on his route, run around the block in
order to reach the end of the alley before he did, and
get a look at his face before he knew what was happening. If that failed, I would have to climb a tree,
yell at him, and solve the mystery when he looked up
to see what was in the tree. (I had achieved some
minor fame as a spy earlier in the summer by discov-
ering a group of older kids trading peeks at various
anatomical details, and charging them a quarter each
to keep my mouth shut.)

The plan was simple, and a failure. Both times I
found myself unable to look at his face. I was fright-

ened. I decided that if no one knew what he looked like, there must be a reason. Either he was so horribly ugly and deformed that my heart would stop or there was something so secret and so sinister about his past that he was hiding his face from all men, and if I saw him he would kill me. I think this was the period I read a good many Nancy Drew, Girl Detective books. Whatever the reason, I didn't look at his face. But I came close enough to realize that he didn't smell bad at all; he smelled sort of like clove chewing gum and chicken feathers.

I began to follow the Garbage Man around town. Sometimes I would stalk him like a real detective, sometimes I would just run around and pop up at the end of alleys until I got bored. Sometimes I would follow him home, and watch him feed his chickens. I decided the chickens were pretty ordinary, and had nothing to do with the main plot. They were part of his masquerade. His house was fairly mysterious, an old two–story frame house which hadn't been painted in years. But why did an old man living alone have such a large house? Was someone held prisoner? Was the treasure so vast that it required a building bigger than the Converse County National Bank?

After weeks of skulking around after the Garbage Man I still hadn't seen his face. But careful questioning of a certain source (my father) had revealed the fact that he had been in town since before World War I, and that there had been "some trouble" because the Garbage Man had a German surname. In fact, his wife had left him, taking their son, and the old man had been a little queer ever since. My informant also stated that some fools had gotten drunk one night and tried to burn down the old man's house, because he "wasn't American." But it all cleared up, and now no one minded that he stole their garbage to feed his chickens, and sold them the eggs.

The Garbage Man began to look for me but because of his posture (his shoulders were on a level with the top of his head and he had a sort of hunchback, not really, but the kind of humpback people get when they are old; not the kind you rub for good luck) I still never saw his face. He would stop suddenly in the middle of an alley, and stare up at the trees, looking for me; or turn around at the sound of running footsteps. Since I never taunted him with the Garbage Man jingle my motives for following him around must have remained totally mysterious. He began to vary his route, something that had never happened in all those years and was enough of a happening to cause talk around town. People talked about the Garbage Man who hadn't thought about him in years, because they were made uncomfortable by his changing his routine.

It became a game, the rules developed without any communication between us, for me to be at the end of an alley before he could stop me and change his direction. Or he would not appear on his rounds at the regular time, but would suddenly turn up in the alley (step, clump! and slide) at twilight or dawn when I was inside. This elaborate hide-and-seek went on long enough for my sisters to begin teasing me about my "Garbage Man boyfriend." At first I was so embarrassed I decided to stop my investigation, but when my mother expressed concern about the amount of time I spent following the man around, and questioned me very closely about my motives, I decided that there must be something going on if the adults were worried and suspicious. My mother came close to ordering me to stop, but I quickly evaded the issue.

I finally had to tell my oldest sister that my reason for following the Garbage Man around was because I wanted to see what his face looked like. She hooted and made faces for a few minutes, while I carefully kept my face innocent and clear. I didn't want her to know the real reason was that I suspected him of being a secret millionaire, with thousands of dollars hidden in that old firetrap of a house. The money, I figured, had to be in gold bars so he wouldn't have to worry about a fire. And he only scrambled through town garbage cans so that people wouldn't know he had so much money; he wasn't a real miser, just careful. And if I could get to be his friend, maybe, well, maybe he would let me see the hidden network of tunnels he had under his house to get the gold inside without anyone knowing . . . but first I had to see his face, so he would know he could trust me because I wouldn't tell anyone what he looked like. It was very hard to keep my face straight and not reveal what a fantastic secret I had.

Mickey soon tired of teasing me and decided to take my problem seriously. Since she was six years older, she had that much more experience fooling and evading adults, and came up with the perfect plan: All I had to do was hide inside one of the garbage cans — and when he lifted the lid, I would have the perfect chance to see his face. Mickey thought he would probably be so ugly that I should have a backup team, in case I fainted from fright and risked being picked up and thrown in the town dump. So she did a little recruiting; two of the Dixon boys for scouts, to let me know when to duck down in the garbage can; my sister Carol to run and tell my mother in case of attack or fainting spells; and herself to direct all operations. I was a little uncomfortable about all the extra troops; somehow, it made the Garbage Man less real, and it seemed to break the rules of my game. But by this time things had gone so far that I had to go along with the plan; Mickey *was* six years older.

> *Garbage Man, Garbage Man*
> *He ain't got no pension plan*
> *Steals his meals from my ash can . . .*

That was the Dixon boys warning me that the old man was approaching. Mickey stuffed my head down in the can and slammed down the lid. I could hear her running over to join Carol near the box elder hedge in the McKibben yard.

It was the McKibben garbage can; I had known the family for years, never been close to them, and there I was alone with the smell of their garbage. It just smelled like regular garbage. Sometimes we went up to the town dump with our .22 rifles and shot rats; the garbage can smelled the same as the dump when it wasn't burning. It was fairly dark inside the can, just a little light from around the lid where it didn't fit tight. This was the first year we had to have lids on our garbage cans, because of the polio scare.

Step, clump! and slide. Step, clump! and slide. Here he came. I would of rather been at High Mass on a blistering July day than inside that can. He was too close for me to run, too close for me to want to hurt him, too close for me to sneak away without being labeled chicken, too close for me . . . what if I scared *him* to death? No one would miss him but me, I'd have to bury him and wear black, and everything, if he left me the money.

The sun came sliding in so fast I didn't have time to blink. And the Garbage Man reached inside to rummage through the McKibbens' garbage before he took a look. Old dry skin, calloused fingers, like chicken talons, touched my arm.

Before I had time to scream, or he had time to know it was me, we both hollered and jumped. The garbage can fell over, the Garbage Man began to run. The Dixon boys ran after him, and back again to ask if they ought to tackle him and hold him for the sheriff. Mickey and Carol ran out from behind the box elder and tried to separate me from the garbage enough to tell whether or not I was killed. And Mrs. McKibben ran out of her house with a broom, yelling at us all to clean up the mess we had made in her alley. The Garbage Man disappeared.

By the time all the uproar had settled, I had run away to hide in a secret tree house in the tree behind the garage. High up in the green and blue world, with the tiny beginnings of apples on the branches around me, I cried. He hadn't been ugly or mysterious — just a regular old face, with bags and wrinkles and interesting bumps and spots. His eyes were bad; all red and runny, one of them half closed and the other popping out in compensation. It was just an old man's face. No mystery, no secret; just an old man's face.

Carrie and Willy, Old Jim Crowe, the Garbage Man are examples of how some people who are "old" live in our society. As a youngster, I was probably closer to them than to my parents, partly because they either told marvelous stories, or by their silence allowed me to build elaborate fantasy worlds around their being. Most of all, they seemed to have time for me. The very young and the very old reach quick understanding; both groups recognize their dependence on the middle generation — for food, clothing, shelter — and have an ability to escape from these kinds of everyday concerns into the world of the imagination. With the old, escape often takes the form of preoccupation with what has passed, with history. With youngsters, their escape is into some unknown future, with daydreams. In some families (or groups or societies or cultures) the old and the young form an alliance within the larger family. For example, I thought my parents extremely dull in experience and life-style compared with my grandparents. I thought they lacked sensitivity and spirit because they were preoccupied with mundane matters like the care and feeding of seven children. But with the old people I knew I could relax and enjoy their company and their stories.

I would sit and listen for hours to Willy telling how the West was won. Movies and books paled next to his vivid accounts; Willy's stories were real, a *lived* history *shared*.

I know I totally respected the old people of Douglas, Wyoming, because of a sense of their history given me by Willy. They survived blizzards, buzzards, land sharks, drought, cyclones, flash floods, the government, and each other; all the disasters imaginable to God and man. And they built a town in the middle of the prairie, a place where children grew and played, nestled in the curve of the North Platte River. I learned about Women's Rights from Granny; about Grace from Carrie; about the pure love of creation from Granddad.

I am an adult now, what my doctor calls a "rapidly deteriorating specimen." And I miss that special relationship between youth and age. It seems to me that the old and the very young understand and accept limits in ability; they have tolerance and patience to spare for small failures. My parents — and teachers, and the parish priest, and all adults — made demands on my behavior that would have been unthinkable among those my own age or among the old people I knew. Elaborate rules of behavior and rigid requirements seem silly to the very old, because they have less time for nonsense. And to the young, constrictive, restrictive, proscriptive forms of being are both artificial and easily forgotten. The old and the young respect one another's frailties for what they are: part of being human.

My "contract" with old people — the unsigned, unspoken ways we developed in the course of a relationship — was always freer, more open-ended, more flexible. It was an agreement to make no demands on each other, just shake hands and see what would happen. When I was very young, and old people seemed much older, I could make such a contract. Now it is harder for me. I am much more a part of the larger American Culture. I find myself regarding old people as pitiful or, worse yet, as a social problem. Now that I approach my middle years, I wonder . . . What To Do With The Old Folks.

Four

T HE fact is, most "old folks" survive about like
they always did. There are a few differences;
the trend away from self-employment means that
seven out of ten workers retire at sixty-five. Most
people hold jobs with built-in rigidity: compulsory
retirement and inflexible retirement plans. Our
grandfathers were farmers, small businessmen, and
so on, who tended to retire gradually if at all. They
managed to remain economically independent during
their old age, and they had large families, which provided another kind of insurance against having to be
dependent on public charity. Today, economic security is based less on accumulated savings and more on

government and company-union pension plans. Families are smaller and more scattered and cannot be counted on for much financial help. With the breakdown of the extended family, and with families living in small apartments or efficient ranch style homes, which seem designed to hold only two adults and two or three children, there is just no space for Grandpa.

Of the total twenty million aged in our society, only 7 percent live in any kind of institution. Sixty-three percent still live with their families, mostly with their spouses or with children. The remaining 30 percent live alone or with nonrelatives. Most of those living in the community are functioning well, and go out without difficulty and care for themselves.

If it is true that these are the facts, that the vast majority of old people remain fairly independent, both physically and financially, what accounts for the picture most of us carry in our heads of the typical old American? Pure prejudice? Youth chauvinism?

When I first began to think about writing something about old people, I approached the subject with the old muckrakers, the crusaders, marching at my side. I was going to *do* something *for* old people. Now it seems I am just acknowledging old debts.

I noticed something else. When I talked to my friends about the idea, they — without exception —

said something like, "How nice. But old people are so boring, so *old* . . ." and then with a sudden brightening ". . . but you ought to meet my Great-Aunt Sadie, or Grandma, or Uncle Joe. They are just marvelous. So well preserved, so young in spirit, so independent, even if they are eighty-seven and have one foot in the grave . . ."

Almost everyone has someone they know, they love, who is also old. But they regard these loved ones as rather special cases. They may be the rule rather than the exception.

In a hill town in eastern Kentucky, I met an old woman called Granny Sukie. She was over a hundred years old, according to her family, and now spent most of her time wrapped in a quilt, sitting by the fireplace in the winter and on the porch in the summer. Granny Sukie was cared for by "Aunt" Mary; Aunt Mary was not any blood relation to Granny Sukie, but considered kin by marriage. Aunt Mary was pushing seventy when I first met her, and she told me she had been caring for "the old lady" for thirty years. Their relationship had begun quite naturally: Granny Sukie needed someone to care for her, and Aunt Mary needed somewhere to live.

Granny Sukie was blind now, had been for many years. But she knew her way around in the way only

a woman who has cleaned and scrubbed every inch
of space can know a house; and she knew every tree
and shrub in the small yard the same way. She had
planted them, had nurtured them, had watched them
grow. Even though she could not see any more,
things were enough the same that her step never fal-
tered.

She told me one day, "The last years of a woman's
life should be spent in trying to settle what's inside.
Early on a woman is so filled with things outside —
her looks and her husband, and her children and her
home — that she never has a chance to be just private. I've had more private time, now, than I need;
but I value these years all the same. I miss readin'
and I wonder sometimes if the hills have changed
any. I've buried two husbands and three children
. . . right up 'til now, my life's been good. But I
wonder if Aunt Mary is gonna last long enough?
Seems to me her arm feels thinner, and she isn't moving so quick. If Mary goes, I haven't much kin left
. . . and if she gets sick, well, can I take care of
her?"

Her face was so full of wrinkles and folds that
sometimes I thought it would look the same upside
down as right side up. Being blind has made her face
appear eyeless, as if a sculptor's thumb had been
drawn from temple to temple, leaving only a continu-

ous deep crevice. She was tiny, so tiny I wondered if she would just shrink away. Compared to her body her hands seemed outsized. They were still the hands of a homemaker; large, with red knuckles, the skin tightly drawn from washing clothes by hand with lye soap. Sometimes her hands would reach out as if looking for a job to do, a baby to bounce or a coat to mend. These hands weren't used to being still. But now she spent her time dozing in her chair, wrapped in her quilt (she could tell stories about each of the pieces in the quilt. It was very old, so old that even Aunt Mary didn't know whether or not the stories were true) and living in a "private place" in her mind.

Granny Sukie and Aunt Mary lived on a stipend from the state welfare office called Old Age Assistance. At the time, for the two of them, they received about $180 a month. The house was owned "outright" but they paid for taxes and insurance. The utility bill was negligible, since they cooked just one big meal a day on the old wood stove, and used very little electricity, because they went to bed with the sun and rose with the dawn. They managed, with the small vegetable garden and a few pretty sad-looking chickens, to eat fairly well. Neighbors frequently dropped over fresh bread, or a pie, as was the custom in that part of the country. In fact someone came by the house nearly every day, just to check on the old women and see that they were all right. They still had some family. They were as rich in resources as they were in years.

Some bright young man at the bank noticed one day that the signatures on the welfare checks were identical and he called the welfare bureau. That office failed to receive any response to repeated requests that the old ladies explain themselves. A team of investigators was sent to the little house.

Aunt Mary was, quite properly, furious that someone would suspect that she was trying to cheat Granny Sukie. She straddled a worn spot in the linoleum, looking for all the world like an ancient sea turtle, her head darting from side to side and her eyes shining, and her low-built, almost legless body never moving an inch. Damn right, she signed both the checks. Did those fools in that office think the old lady could read and write, her with no sight for thirty-more years? She always knew those Ladies Aid women or social women or whatever you called them wouldn't give something for nothing. What did they want? The house? Granny's jewelry? Were they going to send her, send Aunt Mary to jail, so's they could come and drag Granny away and take it all? You never got something for nothing, she knew it, always knew it, shouldn't have started accepting the money in the first place. Well, she'd pay back every last cent. She'd never done nothing dishonest . . .

Aunt Mary against the society of social officialdom was something to see. She had done nothing wrong and that was that. "They" had offered *them* the money; a busy woman with a leather case like a man's came out one day, years ago, and filled out some papers. The money came to the letter box every month, and once in a while some snoopy lady would come and ask questions, refusing tea or any refreshment like she was too good . . .

Social officials were simply routed. First of all, Aunt Mary had no idea of their existence. She wouldn't talk to them. And secondly, to stop the checks now would mean someone had been making an error every month for years. So the old sea turtle beat the great black birds. In the little house in the gentle hills, things go on much as they have for years. Agelessly aging.

The economic aspects of aging are complicated and almost impossible to separate from social and political problems in the community. How can a community support the nonproductive members — providing health services, housing, income, to dependent children and old people — when the proportion of dependent to productive people continues to grow?

How do we balance the need to protect and nurture the helpless against the limited resources of the community? It is considered shortsighted and harmful to reduce the amount spent on the health, education, and welfare of children; but cutting corners on spending on old people is common.

Economy measures in so-called welfare budgets hit the elderly first, hardest — and silently. The old try to survive by cutting corners — eating less, giving up small pleasures like tobacco and movies, doing without warm clothes — and pay the price of ill health and a shortened life-span.

There are many contradictions in our welfare system. One is the fact that when social security benefits (money which comes from funds contributed by all wage earners, and paid back after retirement) are increased, special welfare supplements are cut. Thus the total income of a person is usually decreased.

Old people talk less about the past than they once did; they don't have the time. They have to worry too much about the present. With fixed incomes, declining purchasing power, and increasing need for expensive medical care, they talk about money. One day when I was eavesdropping my way around the Port Authority Bus Terminal, in New York, where many old-timers go in the winter to keep warm, I heard a woman tell a friend that her social security check had been increased from $108 a month to $120; but a $34 special medical grant she was receiving was dropped. She was eligible for the special benefits because the year before she lay near death after having her gall bladder removed, and required a special diet. So our society spent thousands of dollars on her hospital care and she recovered, only to find she can no longer afford the things she needs to keep healthy.

Most old people feel they can manage because they always have. One old man said he tried to save for a rainy day but couldn't. Now if it rains he expects to drown but will swim as long as he can. He is a real representative of the older American; he understands that in the United States the ideal is to work dawn to dusk and pay your own way. If you can't, you are an embarrassment. Yet that old man had worked all his life and contributed his labor to society. He doesn't want "charity"; just enough to live in his last years with some dignity. So, he tells me, this winter he'll do without heat, eat less often, and on his $108 a month he may last until spring. Maybe by spring, this advanced society will increase his check. Maybe.

In the meantime that old man and others like him, all over the country, find no peace, no time for "retirement." It is a full-time job to be old and poor.

I decided to spend some time in the hotel because of the sign painted on the building: PENSIONERS WELCOME. For a long time, I thought that was the name of the place; later I found that it meant they would accept pensioners as lodgers. Not provide any special service or anything, just that the hotel would tolerate old men and women as lodgers. The hotel itself was located in an unlovely section of a singularly unlovely city. The city had been voted an All-American City in recent years, and it certainly had everything all American cities have. Including a rundown town section, located near the jail and courthouse, and full of small hotels, greasy spoons, liquor stores that advertise specials on Muscatel and Tokay wines, and an overwhelming feeling of decay.

If the owner of this particular hotel had any sense and any insurance coverage, he should have been out looking for a good arsonist. The building was structurally sound enough; at least, it didn't lean or anything, and seemed to have been built by honest labor. But the minute you walked inside the door you could smell it, feel it: That place couldn't be saved. There are some buildings where too much has happened, where the walls just can't support any more life. Those buildings are usually in urban centers and are usually eventually abandoned. They are full, finished.

My own mood as I walked down the street was like that of the hotel. I felt finished, depressed, abandoned. I had just begun research on the problems of old people, had spent three weeks working in a nursing home, and a month as a visiting nurse, and was very full of other people's misery. My marriage had been declared a disaster, and I had lost a husband, two kids, a home, a dog and a cat so fast I was just beginning to come out of numbness into the real despair. Sometimes I wanted to kill, sometimes I wanted to die. I had been able to sit for hours, for days, without moving, just staring straight ahead. Now I was trying hard to "pull myself together" and "come out of it" and "straighten UP." I felt just like the old people I was trying to understand. Sick and lonely and wondering if it was worth the trouble to take another breath.

The carpet in the lobby had once had an elaborate pattern, maybe even colorful, like that found in old movie theaters. Time and dirt had erased everything but shadows. It was the same with the rest of the room; everything was colorless, shabby, lifeless. There were places in the carpet where a certain brightness in the pattern suggested the past presence of some piece of furniture, but now there were only a few uncomfortable chairs and the clerk's desk in one corner. A few old men sat around, successfully blending in with the walls and furniture. They looked gray, uncomfortable, unfriendly.

I walked in carrying my own burden of loneliness. It seemed like an appropriate place for me, at the time, even if I wasn't a pensioner. I needed a totally new and undemanding environment. I wanted to be someplace where nothing reminded me of normal happy things; someplace where a deep, ragged sigh would not sound unusual. The lobby was still, so quiet it seemed to be waiting for a sigh or an earthquake or a thunderstorm. It was an empty quietness, somehow; not the quiet of content or the stillness that follows good conversation, but just the absence of sound.

The desk clerk was a hostile cretin. He did not talk but interrogated. Was I from welfare? From the state? The city? What agency did I represent? Who was I investigating? Anything I wanted to know, I could ask him. No sense bothering the old fools. Was I a cop? Maybe some kind of Fed? Well, what did I want?

"A room. With bath, if you have it."

The clerk was not accustomed to listening, unless it was through a keyhole. Direct human communication seemed impossible. His face was webbed; in fact, the wrinkles were so dense that it seemed all expression was caught in a net.

"We don't handle day trade, lady. This here is a resident hotel. But maybe we can make a deal . . ."

Behind me I could feel ears straining to hear every word. I began to realize that the desk clerk knew of only two kinds of young women who would come to that hotel: social workers and hookers. Either way, he was out to make a buck, as long as he was protected. I knew I was blushing and embarrassment made me angry. He had rooms available; I had seen the sign in the window. He was also the kind of person you couldn't let get by with anything. He was a small-time, small-brained creep; but he would be capable of sneaking up to my room with a passkey, or peeking through the keyhole, or making a grab as I walked by . . I almost left the hotel. That desk clerk was like every petty bureaucrat I've ever met; a little power, a little authority, some kind of soft job, and they turn into twisted, grasping creatures. There had never been any beauty in his life, and he would stamp out any he found around him. Any sign of weakness and he would attack. He probably soured his mother's womb.

Anger was a dangerous emotion for me, because I was so hurt and confused over the direction my life was taking, I could not control rage. I would have cheerfully murdered that man, and something in my face must have frightened him. I repeated my request, quietly, not daring to look into his face because of my own anger, and he quickly closed a deal. A room, shared bath, two weeks in advance, forty dollars. He overcharged me.

As I closed the door behind me, I almost regretted my persistence. I didn't mind being considered a dirty young lady as much as I minded living like one. I knew country poor, but not city poverty. The room was about eight by ten feet, just large enough for a bed, a bureau (the top covered by the scars of lonely drinking bouts, hundreds of circles left by wet glasses, and the edge marked by forgotten cigarettes), and a straight-backed chair. The room wasn't noticeably clean, but someone had been very generous with some kind of scented spray. No obvious signs of insect occupation. It was a tiny, smelly, ugly room.

I was also worried about my motives for being there. I wasn't particularly interested in social reform, and I wasn't a reporter. I liked old people, and was interested in the problems of aging, but I didn't intend to make it my life's work. I had thought about writing a book, about organizing old people as a revolutionary political force, because it seemed to me they were natural revolutionaries. They had time, and nothing to lose. But most of this was speculation, idle thoughts. Why was I here in this pensioners hotel, populated by forty or so old, poor, independent people?

Why was I there? Partly, the atmosphere of the place suited me. Like the old people there, I guess I felt more abandoned than independent. Oh, I could manage. But it wasn't as if I had a choice, really. The place was right for me and for the old people who lived there. It was a kind of junkyard for rejected human beings.

When I had left the lobby to come upstairs the room had been buzzing. The conflict and hatred between myself and the clerk had been quite obvious. I hoped this would make the old men feel they could trust me, but I had no idea how to approach them. I felt stiff, awkward; I didn't know the rules observed by people who lived this way. I didn't want to hurt or embarrass anyone, and I couldn't afford to be hurt or embarrassed myself. I couldn't offer to pay someone to let me follow them around. (Excuse me, sir. I am doing research on dirty old men. Could I step into your shoes for a week? For a price? No? Why not? Because, even here at the bottom, you have a right to privacy and a right to choose your own company. Right, sir.) Well, I would just have to approach someone, but not in the hotel. I felt they might be more friendly outside, maybe in one of the local diners or something.

I met Harry and Al over a saltshaker on the corner. They were both old men in their seventies, old enough and tough enough that they remain difficult to describe. They looked alike, stringy in body and sour of face with eyes that were never still. After a while I noticed that Harry did most of the talking, because Al seemed to have a slight drool, perhaps the result of a stroke. They had both been drifters since the Depression, that economic earthquake that displaced so many Americans and left an entire generation scared and insecure. Harry and Al, though ancient, retained the moves of much younger men; like good athletes they had learned to care for their bodies, to conserve their energies, to keep moving. I was impressed with their strength from the very beginning. They had nothing, hadn't ever been much, loved no one, and regretted nothing. They accepted things in a way that was difficult for me to understand.

Harry and Al didn't exactly seek my company, but they agreed to spend some time with me after I convinced them I sincerely believed they had something to teach me, that I wasn't trying to cheat them, and that I wasn't any "do-gooder" either. They were pretty contemptuous of the human race in general, not having generous natures themselves, but were especially suspicious of "guv'ment do-gooders." I think their final analysis of me was that I was a fairly harmless crank.

That first afternoon we spent in a nearby park. They had one bench they always sat on, close to the street so they wouldn't lose the comforting smell of the city. Both men hated the country; they distrusted anything that looked too close to the earth. I would lie in the grass and they were both convinced I would die of worms or some other dread disease. They never saw any contradiction between this and the fact they continually itched and scratched from various bug bites.

We agreed to meet in the morning outside their room in the hotel. I glanced in when Harry opened the door; the room was like a disorderly grave. It was so small they had to turn sideways and scuttle to move between the beds; they had no bureau, and clothing was simply tossed in piles around the room. Everything seemed both dusty and water-stained, like a very old and slightly leaky tomb. They wore the same clothing every day. It never seemed to get any dirtier or cleaner; maybe they each had several outfits in the same stage of filth and disrepair.

A day with Harry and Al always started with coffee and a donut from a diner twelve blocks away, to which one walked. Twelve blocks, in the morning, before coffee. All three of us would silently move down the cement wrapped in our own misery. I felt sorry for myself. Harry tried to move in a way to minimize the pain in a bad knee. Al would blink, blink, mutter and wipe his mouth every fifth step. The reason we went twelve blocks was that in that diner one could buy day-old pastries. Fifteen cents fresh, seven cents day-old. Coffee ten cents, refill for a nickel. That was breakfast. No talking. Everyone in the diner was in the same state of early morning sorrow, that moment of gathering strength to face a day over which one has no control. You have to be ready for anything, surprised by nothing.

Neither man was on any kind of public assistance. Al insisted he was not eligible, had tried to get aid and been turned down. Harry didn't say much but my guess is that he had some reason for failing to apply; maybe a family abandoned somewhere or jail time not yet served. Their days were spent scurrying around the city, like chiggers under the skin of civilization. They lived by panhandling, petty thievery (mostly shoplifting), and occasionally taking a job "on the docks" or washing cars or with a moving company that hired day labor for a buck an hour, a quarter kicked back. In my honor they freelanced a few days. They showed me how to work a street: At the stoplights, they would each rush a car, preferring two women or an older couple, wipe the windshield, and ask for money. Refusal meant they had a right to hurl unspeakable obscenities in the "customer's" face. Working the street usually meant more money than just straight panhandling, but sometimes you would be hassled by the cops. And you didn't do it when high school kids were on their way home. (Both men were terrified of teenage males. It was an almost mystical terror, like primitive devil fear. They would rather be hassled by cops than by teenage boys.)

I tried panhandling. I was terrible at it. Harry said I asked as if I expected to be refused, and didn't deserve any help. He was a master. He could make himself look older, yet still proud. He would shuffle up, planting himself in front of the "mark" as if by accident, and say, "I's old, cold, hungry. Can't work, bad knee. Could you give me a little change to get to the Veterans Hospital?" It always worked. I think Harry usually chose to ask older affluent men, men who were facing the fact of their own retirement and old age. They would give him money just to get him out of the way. Al would hit on women. With his drool, and slightly lopsided appearance, he frightened money out of them.

Actually, I think they preferred to work rather than panhandle. But some days, physical labor was impossible for them. So they would beg. Or steal. One of the reasons Harry and Al finally accepted me was because I was a better shoplifter than they were. They were obviously out to steal. I could go into one of the big supermarkets, pass for a shabby student or maybe a sloppy housewife and come out with enough food for lunch every day. I also tried to get them some new clothes — shirts, sweaters, underwear — but they promptly sold everything I gave them.

We lived in a pretty tight little world, the three of us. I began to find myself neglecting to bathe at night, and leaving my hair in braids instead of washing it. Since we did the same thing every day, I wore the same clothes. Just like Harry and Al.

People would really stare at the three of us. At first I was self-conscious, but I learned to stop *feeling* their eyes. I didn't need anything from them, and they didn't need anything from me. Just like Harry and Al.

We shared a boundless contempt for the hotel clerk. Harry called him the "Gutless Wonder," because he would steal from anyone, even the dying. Harry told me about the man who had been in my room, lived there a long time, slowly dying.

"There lay old Eddy, dying inch by inch, and swearing he didn't want to go to the city hospital. He knew they'd do some awful experiments or something, and he wanted to die in peace. So we would bring him food and medicine. But the gutless wonder couldn't wait to figure what was in it for him. You know how he charges ten percent of value to cash checks? Well, pretty soon, he was taking fifty percent of Eddy's check, plus room rent, plus something for not calling the hospital. And when Eddy died old Gutless stole his clothes. Would have taken his teeth, too, but Joe stopped him. Man oughtn't be buried without his teeth, even if he is buried by the city."

Gutless did steal everything he could. Besides charging me four times the actual rent, he had another small business on the side. Some of the winos in the area would give the hotel as their home address to the welfare office, and their checks would come there. But they preferred to stay on the street or in the cheaper flophouses which were unacceptable to the welfare department. Gutless would report they lived in the comparative opulence of the "Pensioners Welcome" hotel, accept the mail, split the checks with the winos, and everyone was happy. The drunks could afford to drink, welfare could feel they were performing a social service by keeping drunks off the streets, and Gutless had more money. What he did with it was beyond me; he lived in two rooms off the lobby, dressed like the other old men, and was too unimaginative to have any expensive vices.

Since I was able to steal lunch, Harry and Al spent hours in the park with me, just taking it easy, talking about their lives, other people in the hotel, the world in general. Carrie would have said neither man was any better than he should be. They were dirty, suspicious, sneaky, lazy. They didn't believe in God or man or the devil, yet were capable of mouthing the most awful sanctimonious and patriotic clichés. I began to realize they never had an original thought or noble moment. Everything about them — their faces, their bodies, their minds, their souls — was stunted and soiled. They lacked the ability to even *experience* their lives as real. Harry and Al were professional survivors. They saw only what was directly in front of them, they asked no questions, felt no anger, demanded no love; they just made do, just kept body and soul together. They reminded me of nothing more than a couple of antique cockroaches, those marvelous insects that no amount of civilization can kill. Cockroaches survive everything; and so had Harry and Al. But at what a price. They had paid by giving up almost all human softness or warmth. Life had left them somehow degraded. I would sit on the park bench and wonder if that was the only way to survive, if you have to stop feeling anything, stop loving, stop caring, in order to live. It was a frightening thought, but the longer I stayed around the hotel, the more convinced I became that nobody cared.

At the same time, I was aware of the fact that Harry and Al liked me. When I was more depressed than usual, they would try to cheer me up. They would tell horrible corny jokes, and even talk to me in the morning. Their efforts were awkward but they tried to be my friends. And friendship was their one decent instinct. They had total loyalty and friendship for one another. It wasn't love that kept them together, but something stronger. Need. They had met on the road about twenty years ago, and discovered that as a team they were able to survive with less trouble. Two men could cover more ground panhandling, two heads knew twice as many diners where you got bread and butter with soup, not just crackers, two men could work both sides of the street. And if there were two of them they were less vulnerable to attack when tired or weak or asleep.

Their friendship for each other was really the only thing these two had; life had knocked everything else out. I began to be afraid I would disrupt their lives in some awful way, that I was disturbing some precarious equilibrium, some carefully nurtured blindness and insensitivity which enabled them to survive. The other old men in the hotel began to tease them, asking which one I preferred.

One night in the local Mom's Cafe I tried to talk

about all this with the boys. Those "Mom's Cafe" signs mean that for ninety-nine cents you get a complete meal — soup, or salad, meatloaf, potatoes, gravy, dessert, coffee. The soup is watered down canned soup, just like Mom's in the Depression. And the meatloaf is mostly breadcrumbs. But the good places served things hot and gave you extra coffee free. So Mom's was a real treat.

The problem was my inability to accept the responsibility of their friendship. I couldn't guarantee loyalty or support. I was just passing through.

Harry and Al just sat and stared dumbly into their coffee as I tried to explain my problem. They sensed my fear, maybe even before I did. The more I tried to talk the sorrier I sounded. Before long I was ready to cry, ready to say I would take them home and take care of them forever and they wouldn't have to live like this anymore. I don't think I really meant it — I wasn't ready to give that much yet — I just felt so damn guilty about being young enough to leave that hotel and that neighborhood and live another way.

When Harry began to talk his voice was so low I could barely hear. He and Al knew I was worried about them, knew I thought they should be different, better than they were. But they had learned to live one way and that was that. They liked it. Couldn't ask for more, couldn't settle for less. It was their way. But not mine. Besides, they didn't need me, didn't need my sentimentality. They had one another.

Their greatest fear was being so disabled or so sick they wouldn't be able to get on their feet again. Little things they could handle between them, like the days Harry's knee wouldn't work, Al would do the running; but they didn't want to end up a "vegetable."

So like Huck and Tom before them they had cut their thumbs and sworn that if one became so ill that complete recovery was a remote possibility, the other would smother him with a pillow.

After that we didn't have much more to say to one another. That night the bedbugs attacked in full force (I think they knew I was weakened and depressed besides) and I packed my carpetbag and left old Gutless Wonder with two days' rent paid in advance.

Old men. Old women. Almost twenty million of them. Ten percent of the total population, and the percentage is steadily growing. That's a whole lot of people to declare obsolete. In the face of massive public indifference, even rejection, it is amazing the way old people face their days with dignity and strength. They try and remain as independent and young as possible. They prefer to remain in familiar

surroundings, and do things the way they have always done them, because as one grows older, one requires more reminders and signposts along the way
to avoid becoming confused and disoriented. So
sudden changes are something to be avoided; Granny
Sukie *knows* that for her health, and for Aunt Mary's
health, they need to stay in that old and inconvenient
house on the hill. They need the sound of the old
boards under their feet more than they need electricity or plumbing. It isn't just that the old women are
afraid of new ways. It's more like they have to make
so many adjustments to new things (losses of physical ability or the sudden death of an old friend, for
example) that they begin to hoard whatever it is
within us that allows us to face change without seeing it as chaos.

Look at those twenty million old people. They
have been able to go from the era of the horse and
buggy, from a time barbed wire was considered the
most important invention of the century; to hydrogen
bombs and a man hopping around on the moon. On
the moon. And they *do* do it. Harry and Al could talk
about Apollo missions with the same poise they had
when discussing how to hop a freight train or sow a
crop.

Old-fashioned? Never. Old, maybe, but not old-
fashioned. They know about *things;* how to do things,

how things work, even who first did things. Anyone over sixty-five has a more modern mind than I do. They assess and store facts in incredible numbers. I worry about how I *feel* about a machine, like a primitive man; they find out how it works, and handle the mystery with knowledge. The entire life of someone who is old today has been spent mastering technology. I feel defeated by it before we start.

If you are going to be stranded on a desert island, you better hope that at least one person in the group is *plenty* old, because the rest of us have learned very little about survival.

Five

THE artery at her temple throbbed steadily on,
with no concern for the intensity of our conversation, just pumping away, a symbol of both her
fragility and her strength. Steady, sometimes irregu-
lar, beat-pause-beat, I was constantly made aware of
her physical processes, conscious that under her
faintly shadowed blue-white skin — the skin no
longer elastic or protective but just a tissue paper
memory of skin — all of her body struggled to function. I remember once my mother had me feel the
"soft spot" on my baby sister's head. It was pulsing
with new life. How odd to be so helpless, I thought.

With one good poke of my finger she'd be done with. I had the same feeling now.

We — Aunt Jenny and myself — sat quietly sipping coffee as she tried to speak of her life and her aging. I don't know why my thoughts ran occasionally to mayhem, unless it was her total capitulation to conformity. She was so conventional, so polite and did everything with such grace and good taste. But behind all that lay some kind of anger, some kernel of fear and uncertainty, that made her eyes a little anxious and caused her to hold your hand a little too long as you said good-bye. She needed so much reassurance that I sometimes had an impulse toward euthanasia. Who am I? Who will take care of me? Am I doing the proper thing? Am I brave? Am I clever? Aren't I an elegant old lady? Oh, her eyes asked all the questions, even though she acted as if she were perfectly content.

Aunt Jenny was "peaking." There seems to be a particular point reached in lives of old people when they've reached the top of the mountain, when they seem — sometimes quite suddenly and briefly, sometimes for a few years — to see everything with dreadful clarity. All ambition gone, all sense of having a coherent future lost, they have no veils to shield a vision of themselves, their past, the world. Some old people cannot bear this "amazing grace" because it seems to signal their closeness to death. Their minds seem to scramble, rushing from concept to idea to emotion to memory, trying to hold off the visions. But sometimes the grace, the incredible purity of truths and experience is passed on. Aunt Jenny was "peaking" but she was surely struggling to avoid showing it. One simply could not share such profound grief and rage; right up 'til the end, one dressed and ate and smiled and went to concerts, and died without fuss.

Aunt Jenny was a lady of seventy-two quiet summers, vigorous, active and intelligent. She was planning her annual excursion, this year joining an archaeology class from a women's college in France and digging around the summer home of the Marquis de Sade. She didn't enjoy the company of others her age, she told me, they were frequently so boring, so sedentary, so limited in their world view. No, she didn't like being seventy-two years old, and one way to hold off the years was to behave as if it were not so. Everyone thought her quite remarkable, being so adventurous at her age, doing so many interesting things. She felt this was probably her last good year.

"My memory is sometimes bad," she told me. "That seems to bother me more than anything. I can't remember proper nouns — names, places — and sometimes confuse dates. I guess I'm becoming senile. And physically, my brain just seems to *tire* easily. I can't concentrate too long. All those books I bought to read later, all those things I had no time to learn when I was physically active, well, I am still interested, but I just don't have the energy. I didn't think, I never knew, that growing old deprived one of sedentary pleasures as well . . ."

Aunt Jenny is not poor and not alone. She lives in a modern, spacious apartment in New York City, within walking distance of the museums, theaters, shops, and galleries she loves. She is artistic — her home is full of her paintings and sculpture — without the fanaticism of the artist. In another century, if she lost her money, she would have been the lavender gentlewoman who taught painting and piano to sulking girls. As it is, Aunt Jenny's money protects her from judgmental necessity, and she practices her art alone.

Entering Aunt Jenny's world is like being drawn into a gauzy French Impressionist painting. All the colors in her home are muted, almost faded, cool blues and gentle greens. The rooms are full of *things* — paintings, heavy antique silver, Victorian lamps, a baby grand piano — but all are cared for and used. There is no dust on the piano; after thirty-five years of neglect, she has begun to play again. Time and experience has improved her touch, she feels, and the discipline of practicing is keeping her hands supple and strong. The heavy silver bowls and crystal objects are used for family gatherings on holidays. Sometimes, just for her own pleasure, she would set an elegant table and have an elegant meal in solitary splendor. Once Aunt Jenny explained to me that "*things* take a revenge of their own. I collected these things because they were beautiful, or because I needed them to do something, or just because I loved them. Once I had a huge house packed with the things necessary for the wife of a busy, successful man, mother of two lovely children, gracious hostess, sponsor of cultural events — all those roles required so many *things*. So many props. What you see here, this is nothing. I saved very little. But I sometimes feel crowded by all these things. They take up space, time, care, energy. The older I get, the more chained I feel by all this stuff; I don't need it. Maybe I never did. My role required it; I didn't."

When Aunt Jenny speaks now, her voice has a slight tremor and it is somewhat self-effacing in tone, almost coy or cloying. As a girl, she must have been quite attractive because she still has the carriage of a woman confident of her beauty. Now, forming words makes her lips draw together as if held by the hundreds of tiny lines surrounding her mouth.

"I think women became so concerned about remaining youthful after World War Two. Before that, it seemed more natural to be around old people, to see gray hair, to be wrinkled and shapeless and lose your teeth. It sounds primitive, but people usually died before they became too disgusting . . .

"Now I live in an affluent section of the city. And the women around here — women my age — do these amazing things to themselves. Their hair is tinted some pastel color, some color no one was ever born with, and is worn in some style about ten years behind the times. Or maybe they just all wear ten-year-old wigs. And they lift and paint their faces just so, until they peer at the world through a mask. They dare not laugh or cry; all the junk would run off into their collars. I think a woman has a duty to try and be attractive, but a seventy-year-old woman makes a fairly ridiculous imitation of Marilyn Monroe. And the bodies below are clothed in garments far too youthful for most of us. Why do old women feel so pressed, so forced to look young?

"Oh, I know why. Once after my husband died I came back from Europe by boat. And there were many older people on board. But the competition between the women was really quite fierce; every man, young crew members, married men, the captain himself was considered fair game. And all those women simpering, preening, acting like perfect idiots . . . I was ashamed for my sex. But women feel competitive with other women for male attention until death. No dignity, no pride, no independence, no identity of their own. Just desperation."

Aunt Jenny's marriage had been more convenient and comfortable than passionate. She seldom spoke of her husband, more out of sensitivity to the romantic ideal than to any feeling of reticence. She was very moved by the current growth of women's liberation movements; it was as if she had decided men could not be respected or treated as friends, only manipulated and used as a husband-shield, and other women were too dull and boring. So she became an independent woman, particularly able to seek pleasures alone. Even when married she had usually traveled alone, and she chose to paint or sculpt rather than be part of any group. At seventy-two, this sense of herself as able to seek and enjoy things alone was deeply ingrained. It is as if she had had a family (husband, children, big house, PTA, art, some liberal politicking) because in her life and time that was what a woman had to do. The important things in her life, the sources of her strength then and now, are seen by her to be those solitary pleasures.

There is sometimes a look in her eyes of deep sorrow, of barely hidden melancholy. She has an air of nice control, of dreams that are glimpsed but never

seen, of the pain one has when something wonderful
is barely missed. There seems to be a kind of inno-
cence about her, yet underneath I could sense harsh
anger. Her life was governed not by necessity but by
whim — she had the resources to do whatever she
pleased. She also had an overwhelming sense of
"duty" and form. Aunt Jenny was filled with a desire
to know, to live, to do something important, yet her
background and money forced her to confine that
knowledge within, turning always to the hard solitary core.

Sometimes she would sit, erect and girlish, perched
on the edge of a straight chair, and her whole body
would shake with the power of sharing. She would
lean slightly forward, eyes straining and searching,
beyond me, beyond our conversation, trying to tell
the truth perceived in her fraily held state of grace.
Her nostrils would widen, as if at the whiff of the
grave, and the words would tumble out.

"Where is the compensation? What's the *good* of
being old? I love being alive, I want to live fully. But
I just don't see any logic to old age. Being young, being middle-aged, they had rewards, compensations.
You made sacrifices, chose to do without freedom to
have children, chose to marry for love, gave things up
gladly. For all the pain of adolescence, for example,
oh, the joy of being young and learning and growing

and your whole life ahead of you. And every stage of life has pain, hurt, sorrow. But always before, always, there was a balance of joy and happiness. Where is it now? I don't know what to look forward to, or how much time I will have, or how healthy I will be, of what use there is in going on . . .

"I look around at old people — especially people in poor health pushed around in wheelchairs by bored paid attendants — and I wonder why they stay alive. The ones around here have the money to pay for adequate care. Still . . . all that suffering for nothing . . . less than nothing, because they take all that time and energy from younger people to care for them. Why do people have to grow old and useless and draining?"

Whenever Aunt Jenny was most questioning she seemed most alive. She was angry and asking the questions too late. She was near the end of her life and had never experienced magic, never challenged the smell of brimstone, never clawed at the limit of human capability. And now she sat, all good taste and quiet diction, and wondered what it was all about, where it had all gone, how to end it in quiet dignity. Dignity.

"Sorrow. I feel sorrow, but I don't know how to express it anymore. When I was a girl, we used to attend an Orthodox synagogue. And people would weep — actually scream and wail at the heavens. Sorrow was let out, set free, shared. But now, oh, I don't know, it's been trained out of us. Emotions are too private, sorrow a burden too heavy to share. I'm afraid I sound old-fashioned but I'd like to weep and wail like that. Just once, scream my head off for everything I missed and wanted and lost and haven't done. Now, at seventy-two, I tell you I usually feel contented. It's better if I feel contented. But sometimes I am so full of sorrow . . ."

Oh, Lady Jenny, I can feel your grief, hear your questions, admire your anger. But all the questions have come too late. You've led a conventional, blameless, graceful life. The tally sheet is heavy on the plus side; your children are successful in their fields, your grandchildren love you, your husband died without doubting his life. You've always done the right, the proper thing. I don't know why it makes you sad now, I don't know why or how you missed something, missed by so small a margin as to give you a little taste of it. You possess great dignity, Aunt Jenny, even if it is just the cloak you wear now to hide the questions old age brings you to ask. You have health, wealth, freedom. Must your old age have a purpose also? Why now? Why expect a reason for living now? Isn't it enough just to be able to gracefully play the role you have chosen for these last years?

Six

LETTY the Bag Lady lived in a "Single Room Occupancy" hotel approved by the New York City welfare department and occupied by old losers, junkies, cockroaches and rats. Whenever she left her room — a tiny cubicle with a cot, a chair, a seven-year-old calendar and a window so filthy it blended with the unspeakable walls — she would pack all her valuables in two large shopping bags and carry them with her. If she didn't, everything would disappear when she left the hotel. Her "things" were also a burden. Everything she managed to possess was portable and had multiple uses (a shawl is more versatile than a sweater, and hats are no good at all, although she used to have lots of nice hats, she told me). Or was something she had to have, like the oversized leatherette covered Bible occupying a full quarter of one bag, in five-color-illustrated glory.

Letty was pretty crazy and she knew it. I think she even liked being old and frightening. "Scare babies in the womb, I do, this face of mine never was pretty, and time pulls and tugs it in all different directions like an old sweater sagging; and people stop and stare at me in the street. Stupid bastards, I say, someday you'll be old and ugly and hungry. And I'll be among the heavenly hosts, laughing my fool head off — at all of you with your wrinkle cremes and diet soda and wigs and paint. Dead before you live, I say, all of you are dead before you live. Ugly as sin but leastways I had a real life!"

So Letty and I agreed that she was pretty crazy, and she thought I was insane. Should be locked up for morbid interests in old rotten bodies. Tested for queer ideas, and stopped from bothering people. She couldn't accept my simpleminded well-I-just-want-to-know explanation. And if I made things more complicated she'd shake her head and call me a mind-bending fool.

The first day I saw Letty I had left my apartment in search of a "bag lady." I had seen these women around the city frequently, had spoken to a few.

(Including one episode early in my New York City experience when I offered, Wyoming Girl Scout fashion, to carry an old woman's bags. Her response was direct, sudden, and a true learning experience. She whomped me with her umbrella.) Sitting around the parks — Tompkins Square, upper Broadway, Union Square — had taught me more about these city vagabonds. As a group, few were eligible for social security. They had always been flotsam and jetsam, floating from place to place and from job to job — waitress, short order cook, sales clerk, stock boy, maid, mechanic, porter — all those jobs held by faceless people. The "bag ladies" were a special breed. They looked and acted and dressed strangely in some of the most determinedly conformist areas of the city. They frequented Fourteenth Street downtown, and the fancy shopping districts uptown. They seemed to like crowds but remained alone. They held long conversations with themselves, with telephone poles, with unexpected cracks in the sidewalk. They hung around lunch counters and cafeterias, and could remain impervious to the rudeness of a determined waitress and sit for hours clutching a coffee cup full of cold memories.

Letty was my representative bag lady. I had picked her up on the corner of Fourteenth and Third Avenue. She had the most suspicious face I had encountered; her entire body, in fact, was pulled forward in one large question mark. She was carrying a double plain brown shopping bag and a larger white bag ordering you to vote for some obscure man for some obscure office and we began talking about whether or not she was an unpaid advertisement. This immediately caught her interest, because part of her code was that nobody could ever cheat her or take advantage of her. I asked her if she would have lunch with me, and let me treat, as a matter of fact. After some hesitation and a few sharp glances over the top of her glasses (this is at high noon in a big city. I don't know what she was afraid of; I guess I just looked weird to her), Letty the Bag Lady let me come into her life. We had lunch that day, the next, and later the next week.

Being a bag lady was a full-time job. Take the problem of the hotels. You can't stay too long in any one of those welfare hotels, Letty told me, because the junkies figure out your routine, and when you get your checks, and you'll be robbed, even killed. So you have to move a lot. And every time you move, you have to make three trips to the welfare office to get them to approve the new place, even if it's just another cockroach-filled, rat-infested hole in the wall. During the last five years, Letty tried to move every two or three months. "You can't never fix a place up, you know, really clean it or put up curtains and maybe a picture or two because you can't stay, can't get attached. Seems to me I been moving in and out of the same hotel room for the last seven years. Shit-colored floors, shit-colored walls, and the john down the hall a mile, with no lock on the door. Never any time to just settle in, or make a friend. You can't trust anyone, they'll say they're your friend today and to-morrow be pounding you on the head and stealing your things. Like I didn't want to talk to you, you didn't look like a junkie or a pross, but I was afraid you thought I was some rich eccentric, I walk around in these rags because I want to, and the bags are full of money. I been mugged so many times by kids thinking I had money. I may be plenty eccentric, but I sure ain't rich. Maybe I could get a sign or a button like all the kids wear that says I am just as poor as I look, and I look this way because I'm poor. I used to love pretty clothes, I'd save all my money to buy a dress to wear just once. And now I'm lucky to have a change of clothes for the change in seasons."

Most of our conversations took place standing in line. New York State had just changed the regulations governing Medicaid cards and Letty had to get a new card. That took two hours in line, one hour sitting in a large dank-smelling room, and two minutes with a social worker who never once looked up.

Another time, her case worker at the welfare office sent Letty to try and get food stamps, and after standing in line for three hours she found out she didn't qualify because she didn't have cooking facilities in her room. "This is my social life," she said. "I run around the city and stand in line. You stand in line to see one of them new fancy movies with people making love right in front of everybody and calling it art; I stand in line for medicine, for food, for glasses, for the cards to get pills, for the pills; I stand in line to see people who never see who I am; at the hotels, sometimes I even have to stand in line to go to the john. When I die there'll probably be a line to get through the gate, and when I get up to the front of the line, somebody will push it closed and say, "Sorry. Come back after lunch." These agencies, I figure they have to make it as hard for you to get help as they can, so only really strong people or really stubborn people like me can survive. All the rest die. Standing in line."

Letty would talk and talk; sometimes, she didn't seem to know I was even there. She never remembered my name, and would give a little start of surprise whenever I said hers, as if it had been a long time since anyone had said "Letty." I don't think she thought of herself as a person, anymore, I think she had accepted the view that she was a welfare case, a

Medicaid card, a nuisance in the bus depot in the winter time, a victim to any petty criminal, existing on about the same level as the cockroaches.

Over and over again, she would ask me why I bothered to talk to her, and when I said that I just wanted to get to know a "bag lady" she would laugh and say, "Yeah. A bag lady. To you I'm a bag lady."

Letty didn't show for our next meeting. I walked the streets, seeing hundreds of old ladies like her, but no Letty. I didn't know where she lived, didn't even know her last name. There was no way to find her; I couldn't go to the police or any agency. She may have died in one of those weekly fires New York has in old hotels; she may have become so freaky she was locked up in Bellevue. Her body could have been in any one of the alleys on the lower East Side, or she could be buried in Potter's Field.

Wherever she was, I continued to think about her. Tough, mean, ignorant. Formed by her society. But she was still quite a lady, quite a woman. She survived. She managed.

Seven

SHE lives in my neighborhood, a holdover from the days when this block was filled with rooming houses occupied by old people living on welfare. In the last few years, families bought the old town houses, hired decorators and rebuilt the buildings; now tourists walk through the area to see what elegant old New York City once looked like. The old lady treats tourist and resident both with noble hostility and grand contempt.

She hates kids. And can move surprisingly fast on her little gray legs (looking, in fact, like a stick figure drawn by a' sick and hungry child) whenever any child tries to play anywhere on the block. She lives in a corner building and let any unsuspecting youngster bounce a ball, take a piece of chalk out of their pocket, unwind a jumprope, strap on a pair of skates, and she will jump out, shaking her cane and muttering obscenities. Nobody taunts or teases her, either; I think children respect her uncompromising hate of childhood. The lady doesn't mess around. Arms crossed, eyes flickering right and left like those of a wise old snake, she protects her corner from fun and games and laughter.

A real old bitch, she is, hating herself and the world with intensity. I am sometimes tempted to cross the street rather than walk in front of her building, feeling haunted by half-remembered fairy tales. I have tried to talk to her, feeling full of goodwill and noble intentions, and quite sure she will simply have to recognize my charming interest in her. She is quite immune and unimpressed by any approach known to man and regards me with the same air one might view the approach of a thief. She is tiny, stringy, tough; in two years, I've yet to hear her say a pleasant word. Winter and summer she hangs about in front of her building, waiting for something, someone to offend her.

She has one beauty: She is, bar none, the finest shoplifter I have ever seen.

One afternoon, in search of some kind of shampoo

I had become convinced would save me from a fate worse than death, I was canvassing the local drugstores. Since our neighborhood still preserves some of the qualities of old New York, almost every other block has a little drugstore full of treasures dating back twenty years. Finally, I had to go further from home to one of the large chain stores on Sixth Avenue. I had been conscious that the neighborhood viper was hovering about on the edge of my vision in several of the stores, but it wasn't until I reached Sixth Avenue that I began to wonder what she was doing. Was she following me? Would she think I was following her and call a cop? It became difficult to maintain my poise when every time I turned around I caught myself staring into her hard, shifty little eyes. Her eyes had the quality of being deep in color yet suggesting that nothing existed but the hard shiny surface you could see. Looking into those eyes convinced me that living that long could do nothing but pare you down to the smooth hard exterior, destroying all the soft, secret, inner things and leaving a thin shell to walk around as if it were alive.

In the fifth store I finally found my shampoo. The old lady was still there, moving quickly from one area of the store to another, eyes darting around, muttering to herself, her cane knocking down occasional displays and thudding against unwary shins.

She left a trail of confused, irritated shoppers in every aisle. Salesladies rushed to soothe customers, tapping their heads and pointing in the direction of the old lady, making it clear to everyone that she was crazy, pitiful, senile. No one offered to wait on the old lady. It was apparent that people in the store were accustomed to her careening around and disrupting the smooth wheels of commerce. I began to feel a little sorry for the old bitch myself, in spite of the fact I knew she was very capable of taking care of herself. I began to follow her around, with some vague idea of making sure she found her way home.

She moved into another store, a large crowded discount drugstore. Several burly security guards stood around, hired by the manager to discourage all the light-fingered hippies. Knocking a large and elaborately arranged display of aerosol cans of deodorant down in front of one of the men, and moving on muttering, muttering, head swinging from side to side, eyes flashing, a quick turn — and the other man is on his knees picking up gift-packaged, three-in-one, special-today bath powder, cologne, hair spray. Quicker than the tongue of a fly-hungry frog, her old hand flashes out and things disappear from the counter into her pocket. Seconds later another crash, and a startled customer is standing in the middle of various kinds of denture cleaner while the clerk tries to balance a threatened rack of hair grooming aids. Flick, scoop, and another section of the counter glows smooth glass instead of packaged cologne. The clerk turns, eyes sliding across the glass, missing something but not being sure what, hesitates, glances around, and finally moves to rescue the customer. Meanwhile, my old lady had moved on down the aisle and is glaring at a display of cheap toys for children. The clerk apologizes to the customer, moves her finger in a quick circle at her forehead and points at the old lady. Crazy, the gesture says. Poor crazy old goose, she doesn't know what she is doing. Heads shaking, customer and clerk move toward the shining, clean counter top.

The poor crazy old goose moved on through three more large stores, using the same technique. The response in each place was the same, heads shaking in false pity, tongues clicking soundlessly behind pursed lips. The world just didn't appreciate her artistry. In a few hours she had collected enough to change the way she was walking. The booty pulled her shapeless dress even closer to the tops of her high-laced shoes and she leaned more heavily upon her cane. But her eyes kept moving, and her hand flicking out from under her sweater until the profits of every* drugstore in the West Village were considerably reduced. I became exhausted just watching. Finally she turned toward home, and her protected corner. Weighed down with the afternoon's welfare supplement, the old lady came sailing down the street, listing a bit to port because of poor loading. What the old pirate was going to do with all that junk was beyond me. She could have opened her own store with just that afternoon's work. She was obviously tired, yet I didn't dare offer to help. Excuse me, lady, can I carry your stolen goods to the local fence? Let me tell you, I think your method is one hell of a good way to supplement social security, and keep yourself in shape besides. Anyone who could move that fast had no trouble with arthritis; and anyone who could steal in front of television cameras, one-way mirrors, extra security guards, and locked cabinets was obviously not senile.

The next day the fastest hands in town were back on the corner, keeping our block free from the sound of children laughing.

Eight

I knocked on the door for five minutes before I heard footsteps. The card given me by the Visiting Nurse Service said the patient, a Mrs. Vadial, was senile, paralyzed, and lived alone with her husband. She had had a stroke ten years ago and had been visited by a nurse regularly since her discharge from the hospital. The eight-by-five card carried little more information, just listing the services and medications provided.

It was my first day as a "visiting nurse." I was nervous, and had quite deliberately picked this patient as my first; I decided that a paralyzed woman, receiving only token care in the form of regular vitamin shots, would not be much of a challenge. I felt I had to ease in to this sort of work. I was accustomed to working in the fixed formality of a hospital, backed by a hierarchy of diminishing responsibility, where the patient had no control over the treatment or the environment. In hospitals it was very easy to keep your distance, to avoid becoming involved, even to shirk responsibility with impunity. Taking care of people in their homes would be much different; there, the patient at least controlled his environment, and could assume the role of an "employer" rather than a passive victim.

They had told me to wear a dark skirt and white blouse; since I was only a temporary employee, the pale blue uniform of the visiting nurse was an unnecessary expense. My hair was pulled severely back, I had square horn-rimmed glasses firmly in place, and my nursing school pin was prominently displayed on my collar. I thought I looked like a very respectable nurse. I was carrying the large, black, square bag, full of all the things I needed to make the day's calls: medication, syringes and needles, a new catheter for one woman, ointments, bandages, gauze, a blood pressure cuff, a stethoscope, and soap and paper towels to wash my hands after every visit. I remembered the importance of placing the bag on clean newspaper whenever I stopped and hoped I wouldn't

have to ask anybody to provide one. It seemed rather
insulting: Put a newspaper on the table, lady, I can't
carry your germs over to the next house. God knows
what might be lurking around here. I don't know
why, or who, or when, but someone once decided
that a piece of newspaper is apt to be the cleanest
readily available surface in any home.

It's funny, the things you remember. I could remember about the newspaper under the bag, even
though I didn't understand the reasoning behind it,
but I knew I had never learned to give a proper injec-
tion. In fact, I gave the worst injections in the world.
I could pick the precise area, pull the skin taut with
my thumb and forefinger, grit my teeth and try and
remember to snap the needle in, quickly and pain-
lessly. My technique would be impeccable, I would
never contaminate the syringe or needle, I never
made a mistake in calculating the amount to be given
or in the medication to be injected; but when it came
to the point in time when I was supposed to flick the
old needle in, something in me always cringed, always hesitated just that fraction of a second, and I
would know I had messed up again. My shots hurt. I
hated to see the needle piercing flesh, dimpling the
skin slightly and swiftly disappearing. In fact, I had
developed the habit of telling my patients that contrary to popular mythology, my injections did smart a

bit. No little bee sting in my needle; you could feel every little millimeter of needle going into the skin. Oddly enough, I was much better at intravenous injections; maybe because those you have to do slowly and carefully anyway, in order not to miss the vein, while intramuscular and subcutaneous injections should be given quickly in order to minimize the pain. I hoped Mrs. Vadial would forgive my needle complex, and not look at me with the reproachful eyes of one used to more expert injections.

I stood on the porch, looked blankly into the hot California morning, and wondered why the footsteps on the other side of the door were so slow and careful. Perhaps Mrs. Vadial could walk, even if it was a hesitant and painful process. Victims of strokes, I knew, could almost all regain use of their extremities if given proper rehabilitative treatment. Few treatment centers wanted to work with old people, however; it is much more rewarding to care for the young, the crippled football player, the child hit by a car — victims of "real" trauma rather than just victims of old age. I hoped she was one of the lucky ones, one of the very few who receive quick, expert rehabilitation. Nothing is quite so discouraging as watching someone recover some or all of their mental faculties after a massive cerebral vascular accident, only to find their physical abilities permanently impaired through lack of exercise, joints locked by staying in one position too long, muscles atrophied because nurses hadn't time to do passive exercises for the patient while they were struggling to conquer a blood-fogged cerebral coma. I hoped it was Mrs. Vadial on the other side of the door.

Of course it wasn't. I should have known by looking at the neighborhood, a working class area of small private homes with meticulously kept gardens. All of their capital was represented in that property, I was sure. They would not have the money for expensive rehabilitation. Especially ten years ago, before the advent of Medicare and Medicaid. My visit was being paid for by Medicare.

The gentleman who opened the door did not look friendly. He stood impassively on the other side of the locked screen door and refused to believe I was "the nurse." "The nurse" always wore a blue uniform and didn't drive up in a red sports car. "The nurse" arrived every Thursday, promptly at ten o'clock and not this early. "The nurse" didn't look suspiciously like one of those longhairs. I showed him my pin, my license to practice nursing in the state of California, my driver's license with its matching name and picture, and finally the little eight-by-five card with the ten years of care marked in uninformative, unimaginative, medical jargon. Finally, Mr. Vadial opened the door and allowed as how I *was* carrying a bag just like "the nurse." He directed me toward the kitchen, breathing down my neck, never more than a few inches from the strange intruder. Sharp little eyes became sharper as I started to place the bag on the table and remembered to ask for a sheet of newspaper. He relaxed as he spread the paper on the spotless enamel table; I had passed the test. Only "the nurse" would ask for a newspaper to place under her bag.

Mrs. Vadial was sitting in a wheelchair by the table. Actually, to say she assumed the posture of sitting is not quite correct; she was a massive, inert, blob; she looked like a piece of freshly risen dough, molded carefully into the form of a woman, dressed, and pressed into a wheelchair. It was not possible to tell if she was alive except by the rounded chest moving up and down; and who could tell if any intelligence informed her glassy stare? Had she been this way ten years?

Yes. Ever since his wife had suffered her stroke ten years before, in the middle of one of the hottest summers ever in California, she had been unable to speak. She could move her eyes, and the fingers of one hand, so they were able to communicate somewhat. "I know what she wants," he said. "We been together a long time, so I know what she wants. She

likes lots of things, likes good food, television, listens
to the radio, I know. I see her hand move up and
down when the music is good. I give her a bath, we
eat good, and the real nurse, I mean the regular one,
she teaches me things like how to give enemas and
how to move her without hurting myself. Ma, she always was pretty independent and I know she don't
want anyone doing for her but me. I was retired, we
were going to travel a little maybe. But we can't do
that now; riding in the car is no pleasure for my wife.
She likes for me to read to her, old books from her
childhood and the Bible. And I have plenty to do
around the house; I had to learn to cook and clean
and iron and take care of things. Before her illness,
my wife took such pleasure in our little house and
garden, didn't let me do a thing. I was a king in my
house, a gentleman waited on hand and foot. She always said I had worked so hard, I needed plenty of
time to catch up on my rest.

"But now she is resting. Ten years in the wheelchair and in the bed. I take good care of her, you'll
see. No bedsores like she got in the hospital. I had
them take the tube out of her bladder because she
was getting so many infections, and now I keep a
thing like a diaper around her.

"I tell you, I got plenty to keep me busy."

As he talked, Mr. Vadial pulled his wife forward

in her chair, bending her head over her knees and
pulling the flaccid buttocks up in readiness for my
needle. He watched sharply as I prepared the medication, sponged the precise area, got a good grip on
the clammy flesh and tried to remember to snap the
needle in. It's all in the wrist, they tell me, I remember, and I still gave Mrs. Vadial a terrible shot. She
was in no position to complain. That made it more
painful for me, somehow, because I didn't know
whether or not I had hurt her. Could she feel anything? Was any part of her brain not blood-starved
and destroyed?

Mr. and Mrs. Vadial. The little card said they were
both seventy-eight years old. They must have had
little time for the leisure years of his retirement; she
had been like this for ten years. He wasn't very big,
the sort of small, wiry man who seems bursting with
energy and able to handle any burden. She was a
burden, surely, but he seemed proud of his ability to
care for her. With all her unhealthy bulk she must
have been twice his weight, yet he regularly moved
her in and out of bed, kept her dry, gave her baths,
kept her company. Whenever he had to leave the
house he arranged for a neighbor to sit with her. He
was afraid of fire. He was worried about robbers and
about anything happening to him before she died.

I asked him if he had time to give me coffee before

I left, and when he looked startled, realized that was something the "real nurse" would never do. He was deft and quick in the kitchen; I wondered if he had reorganized things or left everything as his wife had wanted it when she provided all the service.

"No," he answered. "I think Ma likes to look around and see things where she last put them. Oh, I changed things a little, so it's quicker to reach, like, but mostly I just work like she did. I painted this room, myself, this year. Same colors. I don't have her touch for decorating and fixing up. When she was around — ain't that right, Ma? — well, everything she touched seemed to take a comfort from her hands and become more fitted in, more complete, somehow. I ain't got that touch. I can keep it clean and nice, though, so's we're comfortable."

We sipped our coffee and talked. The three of us. Mr. Vadial had the habit of including his wife in the conversation, and I found myself glancing at her as if she could understand. She never moved, never made a sound. But I think I began to feel she was listening, and listening with pleasure. Mr. Vadial was so convinced, so sure, she knew everything that was going on around her. And he knew her better than I did.

Their family doctor, several social agencies, and his children had all tried to get the old man to move his wife into a home. My instructions were to ask him if he had reconsidered, and if he had gone to see one of the new nursing homes being constructed just a few blocks away. I didn't have to ask the Vadials what they wanted to do. Any fool could tell she was better off here, with him fussing around, talking to her sensibly, keeping her as well as he was able. She was clean, the house was spotless, and he showed no signs of resentment.

I mean that. I sat at that table for an hour and probed around, trying to find some little part of him that didn't want her, that wanted out, wanted to be free of his fleshy burden. But all I could find were rare gifts in a home. Love, dedication, caring, selfless service. When I left, assuring the old man that the "real nurse" would be back next time, I almost envied Mrs. Vadial. She had herself a real loving man, a man who would never give up, never desert her. Even if she didn't know it, even if her brain was totally scrambled, he was satisfied to serve out a promise made long ago.

He reminded me. "In sickness and in health . . ."

Nine

I remember an old Japanese story about a grand-mother who decides it is her time to go to the mountain. Her family is grown, the hut is becoming crowded with grandchildren, and food is scarce. She feels the call in her heavy legs, in arms no longer strong enough to do the daily tasks, in eyes too weak to sew a proper seam. The knowledge that she is preparing herself for death comes slowly to the family and is wordlessly communicated from the oldest son to the youngest granddaughter. She divides her belongings. She cleans the hut from top to bottom and sees that all is in order. She waits for the first snow to begin falling.

During those days life continues as it always does and as it always will. A child is born, winter wood is cut and stacked. The heavy quilts are aired and cleaned. Everything seems the same on the outside, but the grandmother grows in dignity as the fall turns toward winter. She thinks about her life with quiet satisfaction and smiles to see the children play the same games she played as a child. The time comes, the first heavy flakes of snow fall, and Grandmother goes to the mountain.

Now I must talk about another version of the mountain. The old grandmother of the story had looked at her life and found it good; had looked at herself and found that for her life was complete, a circle drawn, a story finished. She had spent her days with her family, her community, a few friends; had loved and laughed and worked. And when she went to the mountain she walked in the sureness of a life total and complete. She was ready.

Now there is an earlier separation for the aged, an earlier leave-taking to a special place, a place for the old. These are called retirement villages or adult communities and one must be a "senior citizen" to gain admittance. They aren't anything like nursing homes or geriatric wards of madhouses; those are more like death houses for the sick and helpless. Retirement communities are places for old people to live among their peers. They are segregated areas for those over fifty-five or sixty to live away from the sound of children playing, to live without the responsibility of caring for families or houses long emptied of children. One gains admittance by saying yes, I am old, yes, I have nothing to do, just hours to fill. They are communities filled by frightened middle-class men and women who have the money to buy a home — no, a house — away from places and things reminding them of their lost youth.

I can't tell you too much about what life is like in one of those communities, because that is one of the rules. Outsiders, young people, aren't permitted to spend much time inside the walls. I never really got to know anyone who lived inside; the communities are planned for total living so that one need never set foot outside.

They have complete recreational facilities — swimming pools, golf courses, sewing rooms, art studios, even movie theaters and chapels and shopping areas and medical facilities. They have everything an old person should require. Transportation to the outside is provided if one should be so foolish as to need something not provided by the planner; and the director of recreation sometimes even plans a trip to a concert or a beach or a museum. "The Residents" move in groups. The brochures and advertisements for the communities show them playing, swimming, laughing, always with other people "their own age." It is called "Total Retirement Living." It is also total separation from anything not included in the plan, a middle class, country-club atmosphere very different from the austere mountain climbed by the Japanese grandmother.

High stone walls, frugally landscaped, surround the area. There is a gatehouse with a uniformed security guard and a twenty-four-hour security patrol of the grounds. Inside the walls, uniform blocklike houses line the streets, some with carefully kept gardens, some with brand-new seeded lawns. Except for the size of the houses, which varies from tiny to small, the houses look like suburban housing for middle income families in any section of the country: flat, low, lots of wasted space, nothing in the design to please the eye or relieve the monotony. There seems to be a good deal of concrete. The sidewalks are wide, most of the houses have driveways and garages, the streets are spacious. I guess paving is cheaper, requires less upkeep, and can always be explained in terms of special designing for the "Freedom Years."

Mrs. Duffy was posing as my mother, eager to find a permanent, safe home. She had carefully dressed for the occasion: she wore sensible shoes, a flat straw hat, a flowered wash dress, and carried an umbrella. She was fifty-eight years old and felt far too young to be looking at a "Retirement Village." I had tried to look as prosperous as possible but the guard at the gate looked rather doubtful. I thought he was of the opinion that we couldn't afford to buy her freedom in her freedom years.

Mrs. Duffy was plainly awed by the careful planning of the builders. "Here we are," she said, "less than thirty miles from some of California's most beautiful coast, and they build a place that looks like Kansas on the backside of the moon. Good Christ! They have everything lined up just so, even the trees, one on each corner of the house, one at the third crack in the driveway . . . Sweet suffering Jesus."

"Look, Mrs. Duffy. You're supposed to be a moderately wealthy, slightly eccentric, active old lady that I want to get out of my hair. And you're interested in finding a nice place to live with others just like you . . . so cut the swearing. You promised — I don't like it any better than you do — but . . . oh, just help me out. Just try and look at this place like any other old lady and tell me what you think."

I was afraid to approach one of the retirement communities straightforwardly; afraid they wouldn't take to me, afraid they wouldn't let me see things, afraid they wouldn't just let me talk to the residents.

Mrs. Duffy was my decoy, my support, my extra pair of eyes. She was also my friend and resented being called an old lady.

Can retirement really be secure? Mrs. Duffy, my conspirator, was angry at being called old because it made her feel used-up, useless, nonproductive. As we drove toward the manager's office, she became more and more restless, pulling her hat to a more rakish angle, smoothing the skin under her chin, pulling at her dress, freshening her lipstick. I could feel her thinking, I'm not old enough for this place. Not ready to be thrown into the dustbin yet. Why, I don't even like people my own age. She ran a boardinghouse for students and loved to be considered one of the gang. She was never pushy, never forced her company on anyone, but everyone who lived in her house loved her, confided in her, brought her gifts of her favorite plum brandy, and usually stayed around to help consume it. She was a widow, her husband had been a railroad man, and she was the champion of anyone with long hair. It wasn't that she tried to appear young; on the contrary, she was dowdy and comfortable. She just wanted to be part of what was going on now, today; she wasn't ready to add things up and say, well, that is the past, and now I will sit down and think about it until . . .

"You know something about those walls?" she

asked. "I don't think they are to keep anyone out; I think they built those damn things to keep people in! All those stories about concentration camps being built in the United States for radical kids — humph. Here is your concentration camp. For old kids. Keep 'em out of the way. Lock them up, give them a nice place to live, bleed them of all their money, let them play like a lot of children in camp — and boom. One day all these old people will wake up and find out the gates are locked. From the outside."

"I am the village counselor," said the small man in a very shiny suit. "I hope that I can answer all your questions, show you one of our little homes, let you wander around the golf course, the swimming pool, the craft rooms; in short, I am here to help you see our village, but not be in your way. Let everyone make their own decisions, I always say, don't try and push people . . . especially when one is making such an important decision like where to spend the golden years, the years of freedom, the fun years when one can do anything one wants . . ."

"We are interested in seeing all the facilities, and talking to some of the residents, it seems to be such a nice quiet place; just the place for Mummy," I said.

Mrs. Duffy would never forgive me. Mummy, indeed. "How much?" she said.

"I beg your pardon, madam?"

"How much. Money, total, to live here. If I could live here."

"Well, that depends on which model condominium you select. And the location. Well, really, I can hardly talk price when you haven't even seen the product, heh, heh."

We were ushered out of the office and into a golf cart for a tour of the grounds. Mrs. Duffy maintained a tight-lipped silence as I commented on the shrubberies, the grounds, everything so neat.

"Well, we try and keep everything lovely for our residents. Being surrounded by lovely peaceful things is so important; when one is getting on, order and neatness really begin to count."

"Like in a grave," said Mrs. Duffy.

I glanced at Mrs. Duffy, trying to tell her I would personally pour down the drain the three bottles of plum brandy I had used to bribe her, if she didn't become more cooperative. She grimaced, and asked the man, "How much? You still haven't given us any idea how much. And what does it include? What privileges does this owning a con-do-minium guarantee?"

The village counselor smiled understandingly in my general direction, knowing that the children usually sign the papers, convince their parents to move, love the place. Old people are such a problem, his

glance said. Mustn't upset the old lady, must keep
her happy, we'll show her plenty, we'll show her how
perfect a place this can be. "Well, madam, buying a
little home here opens all sorts of new horizons. You
can join any of the craft clubs, use the clubhouse, the
swimming pool, all of our very fine recreational facilities. There is a small charge for guests, of course,
and a yearly fee for the upkeep of the golf course.
But when you purchase a home here you are purchasing a way of life, peace of mind, freedom from
worry about being robbed or bothered. We are all
good people here, fine people, living together in a
planned community for peace and security. The price
of the home is within the market range; in other
words, you pay the same for a new little cottage here
as you would in any of the developments. But here
you have security, and people your own age. You pay
a small monthly fee for maintenance. And then you
are free from worry, free from the duties of mowing
the lawn — why, most of our residents don't even
bother to lock their doors. We have a security patrol,
twenty-four hours a day, just looking after your welfare so you can sleep in peace . . ."

"That's exactly what the man said when I bought a
plot in the cemetery for me and my husband," answered Mrs. Duffy.

We climbed out of the golf cart silently. The building in front of us was the "clubhouse," or recreation center.

The building resembled a small-town high school, built by the mayor's brother-in-law. There was a good deal of native stone, weathered wood, glass, and plastic. The village counselor began showing us all the things one could do during the golden years; the bulletin board had meetings and dances and competitions scheduled for every hour of the day and night. There seemed to be no limit to the number of activities. A lecture on "Group Therapy: Its Goals and Uses" was scheduled for that evening.

Among the score or so residents we saw in the building, most were quietly working at traditional crafts. Women were knitting, mending, talking in small groups. Several men were building a bookcase in the woodworking shop; one man sat in a corner, whittling away just like an old man sitting on a porch. They didn't pay much attention to our presence; tours were always coming through. The workshops were well equipped, light, airy. If some of the products displayed were not to my taste, well, some people like beaten copper reproductions of the Last Supper and hand carved likenesses of Polynesian dancing girls. I don't think the product mattered much; I think most of the people working in the shops were working because they liked doing things with their hands and were accustomed to working.

In another time, another century, the men would still have been active in their crafts; but these men looked like retired businessmen, uncomfortable in their casual clothes, a little awkward with some of the tools, and not particularly interested in the excellence of the finished product. The bookcase listed to one side.

The recreation center was indeed the center; it was the hub of the village, surrounded by all the facilities planned retirement could offer. The golf course, the swimming pool, badminton courts, a lovely lawn with chairs scattered around, all were comfortable, fashionable, clean, and not in use.

"Where is everybody?" I asked. "It's such a lovely day, and . . . well, no one seems to be around."

"Big dance last night, heh heh," said the village counselor. "These old people love to dance. But the next day is always pretty quiet."

We continued our tour. There was a sameness to all the streets, but our guide was doggedly conscientious, telling us about each type of house, telling little anecdotes about the wedding held last week — single men are grabbed up really fast, he said. We have more ladies, you know, and a man can take his pick. Romance blooms in the golden years — and gently questioning Mrs. Duffy about her income, her interests, her health. He was very efficient. I was half hypnotized by the drone of the golf cart, half blinded by the bright sun, depressed by the silence of the streets. But the gentleman soon found out all there was to know from Mrs. Duffy, and pulled up in front of one of the new homes.

"This is perfect. This is you, Mrs. Duffy. There is room for a small herb garden, on the side of the house, it is quiet and not too close to the main recreation area, it is small and comfy. Shall we look?"

Jesus Christ, I thought. What have I done? What if Mrs. Duffy decides she wants to live here, here in the special, plastic, packaged place . . . Maybe she likes the idea of planned retirement. But the thought of my friend, the plum-brandy freak, the woman so many people shared their lives with; lively, beautiful Mrs. Duffy wanting to be closed inside these walls, was unbearable. I understood some of the other people we had seen and talked to. Most of them came from small towns, places where the community was changing rapidly. They had been joiners all their lives, active in fraternal organizations and clubs. They thought the country club atmosphere, twenty-four hours a day protected by security guards, thought it was the only way to spend their time in comfort.

The average American family moves every five

years. They don't have roots anymore. The newer generation of old people, people who are just now reaching retirement, probably have less sense of themselves as part of any community than their children. They have been moving all their lives, looking for the perfect place, the perfect house, the perfect job. Mobility. And retirement communities seem to be a logical stop on that road. The brochures and the sales pitch all promise trouble-free, fun-filled hours, no responsibility, no worries. It sounds like Utopia. Just pay your money and sit back and relax. Do your thing.

So there are twenty million people over sixty-five in the United States right now, and the proportion is increasing. They represent about $65 billion in business; money that they will spend on food, on housing, on medical expenses. The old don't save; they have to spend their money. They are the perfect consumer.

Most of their income will go for housing. And builders recognized a new market. Shazam, and the retirement community was invented. It looks very much like its neighbor, the average American suburban sprawl, but buyers pay for little extras like wider doorways, support bars in the bathrooms, electric stoves, security guards; all those little things that make them feel at home.

I watched Mrs. Duffy walking around the little

house. She was poking around, kicking mopboards, opening ovens, checking closet space. The place was just a box. But I tried to see it as she would, tried to see her things in the rooms, the air filled with the smell of her weekly stew; I wondered if she wasn't very often lonely and afraid. These people were promising security, companionship, and fairly reasonable prices. Oh, the monthly maintenance cost would crawl up as prices outside became higher. But she could just manage, selling her house, using the pension from the railroad, not buying too many new books and records. And she could step outside the door, guaranteed friends, safety, little things to fill the hours.

I left the house, left the village counselor telling Mrs. Duffy about how they were starting a lecture series and needed someone to organize speakers and wouldn't she just be perfect, with all the people she knew at the university, and her taste and intelligence. It would be so nice for all the people in the village to have someone of her ability there to keep them up to the mark, intellectually, you know, lots of them didn't know Bach from Beethoven. She could do so much good . . .

He certainly was a salesman. He knew people, I'll give him that. From the front steps of the house I could see a section of the hills being torn up for more housing. The occupancy rate was almost always a hundred percent, the man had said. People buy as fast as we build. It's the way things are out there, out there in the world. Robbers and dope and hippies and God knows what. Here within these walls, nothing can threaten you. No one can harm you. It's like the Garden of Eden before . . .

I marched to the house next door and demanded of an old man sitting in his garden "Are you happy here? Really? Do you like it, like it so much you wouldn't leave ever, unless you died? Is it a perfect paradise, is it freedom?"

The man never answered my question. Mrs. Duffy came out, followed by a puzzled looking village counselor and we were driven back to our car in silence. Mrs. Duffy had removed her hat and, I suspected, her kid gloves. The gentleman tried to open his mouth several times but, glancing at her closed profile, kept quiet. It must have been very painful for him; I saw him glance longingly at the well-kept gardens, and a small greenhouse. I know he must have had a special speech all ready for this area. I also knew better than to talk when Mrs. Duffy wasn't interested. So we moved jerkily through the hot afternoon, no sound from us, no sound from the village, only the irritating buzz of the electric golf cart.

"Okay, Duffy, what did you do?"

"ME DO?" she shouted. "I didn't do a goddamn thing. But that fool man, and his foolish patter, and his stupid company — what do they think we are?

"Oh, I expect to get cheated a little on some deals. Everyone does; that's almost an American sport. The butcher doesn't give an honest weight, the dentist does less than he charges you for, the plumber puts new pipes where old would suffice. But I hate to be treated like an *old* fool. That place. Bad construction. Cheap fittings in the bathroom. And then he tries to tell you the rooms are larger than they are. 'Yes, madam, all your fine old things would fit here. Why, these rooms are quite large . . .' Now you know that isn't true. They have undersized furniture in those rooms so they feel larger. They have all kinds of fancy tricks to make it look luxurious; and when some poor devil tries to move in with his few things, he'll be crowded out and uncomfortable. So I asked the man, very sweetly, what if I don't bring my stuff? Are there furniture stores? Oh yes, there are, and they sell things just for these houses . . . ugh.

"And the maintenance fee. It's different for the areas, like higher close to the recreation area. But there are little extras mixed in here and there. Everyone is required to subscribe to some fancy health insurance plan. My benefits don't count. Oh, I don't know. They cheat old people. They fancy up the golf course, and the craft section, and cheat on the houses. They charge you for maintenance and encourage you to keep your own garden. What do they want? Why is it so hard to be honest?

"All those old people dancing, dancing, I can see them, swirling around, determined to look like they are having a good time even if they aren't, because they don't want to depress their friends. Square dancing, do-si-do, and hoping it is the last dance, because they must get tired of always having such a good time, of being such good advertisements for the place . . ."

I shouldn't have worried about Duffy; she had a community and a center to her life. As long as she was able, she would run her boardinghouse, drink her brandy, sing the old songs for new generations. And she would last a long time.

There is another type of retirement residence where living a long time is its own revenge. Scores of nonprofit, church-and-fraternal-organization-sponsored, so-called life care institutions for the retired are opening in the United States. The idea has been around for a long time. These "life care" homes guarantee tender loving care for the rest of your natural life, in exchange for some stated admission fee, so much a month (for example, a person's entire social security check) and the signing over to the organization of your entire estate.

The first "life care" center Duffy and I visited was a twin-towered, high-rise building, ultramodern and very expensive. To be selected as a resident, one had to be in good health, pay $40,000 entrance fee, pay $350 a month for a one-bedroom suite, and sign an agreement assigning one's estate (including insurance policies) to the sponsoring church. This "home," because of its religious affiliation, enjoyed special status as a tax-exempt organization.

In return, one was guaranteed total care, including medical care, for the rest of one's natural life. The director called this "part of doing the Lord's work." The building had a well-equipped infirmary, staffed twenty-four hours a day by professional nurses. It was close to several large hospitals and medical centers. There was a chapel and a recreation area on the main floor. Meals were served in a pleasant dining room for those who didn't want to cook in their own apartments. Shopping, a pleasant park, and public transportation were all nearby.

Most of the residents were what I would call the affluent elderly; predominantly female, white, gloved and hatted. They were very pleasant. Everything was very pleasant, even lovely. Heaven on earth, including the relief from the burden of worrying about worldly goods.

Frankly, Duffy and I didn't last long in that place. The manager, with the practiced eye of a good salesman, seemed to know we "didn't belong." We were taken on a brisk tour, given leaflets and brochures, and told there were no vacancies at present. Well, it was a pretty fancy place. But it seemed to me the Lord's work came pretty high.

The residents themselves would probably disagree. They had luxurious, carefree living in the company of others like them; they didn't have to worry about any debilitating illness threatening savings or security; they felt they lived in a safe, secure environment, protected from any wandering robbers, rapists, or other evil forces. They were protected and shielded.

Duffy and I visited several "life care" centers and another "adult community." After each trip, she would be angry and I would be depressed. It's difficult to explain why; partly, I think, *any* person "getting along in years" as Duffy would say, does feel insecure about the future and a little threatened by the present. Even Duffy worried about being ill and unable to care for herself; she had no family, just her boardinghouse and a small pension. Her anger came from feeling slightly tempted to give up her freedom and independence in return for a feeling of security. Yet she could *see* all the defects of these places; she could feel the sales pitch being a little shady around the edges. They weren't for her, but she was still tempted. That made her angry because it was not consistent with her self-image. She was Duffy, independent, feisty Duffy, an original. She didn't belong in a "safe" place; she was strong enough to live in the real world.

And I would be depressed because my objections were so subjective. I just don't like plastic havens. I felt the residents were being conned, kidded into a false sense of security and forced into a world with restricted horizons. All the places we saw were boring. I didn't like the sales pitch, because it preyed on all the fears of the aging person, and promised fences, dances, arts and crafts. It seemed to encourage an early resignation from society, a removal of certain elements from the community, a segregation of the aged.

And that process solves none of the problems of aging: It just improves the packaging. It is a solution without substance and underlines a poverty of imagination. Why should the elderly settle for segregation and idle pleasures? They should demand security, leisure, good health care, housing; but they should be recognized as responsible adults, not foolish children. The aged person should be part of the community. We need them.

I need Duffy, just as she is. And when she gets too decrepit to lift her glass, her community — the people she has loved and aided, the society she lives in — has a responsibility to help her, not put her away.

Ten

WE walked slowly through the pretend garden, just a narrow walk surrounded by tiny evergreen bushes and casually placed rock, nothing colorful, nothing that required the constant care of a gardener. The old woman clutched my arm and begged to be taken back to her room. She was too weak to walk, too tired, she didn't want to be outside. I was younger, stronger, pulling her along, ignoring her plea. She needed to exercise, needed to be out of that place; if she just stayed in bed she would soon die. Walk, I told her, walk. You must get your strength back. Come on, I said, tugging not so gently now and hearing my voice impatient, you simply must move around.

She had been my friend. We had met months before at a lecture when, both bored and feeling guilty (the lecturer had been an honest and righteous man, but cursed with a monotonous voice which drained his words of interest and passion) we had tried to leave the hall without being noticed and collided in the doorway. I had smiled because she looked so startled, like a child caught with forbidden sweets. "It's like leaving church in the middle of a sermon," I said. "You feel you've offended God." We laughed and left the building together.

There was seventy years' difference in our ages. We shared a mild cynicism, met frequently for lunch and tore apart the reputation and motives of public figures. She considered herself a conservative — I was a radical. Nothing ever changes, she would say, you must save the things that are good and familiar, otherwise people become confused and destroy everything. Nobody has ever tried to change *enough*, I would retort. Everything must change if the world is to be a fit place to live.

And so we would talk. She was ninety-six years old. Her passion was bridge. She liked order, quiet, things properly arranged. For thirty years she had taught mathematics to uninterested high school students;

she had never found a pupil, she said one day, who could understand the beauty of numbers, the neatness of problems neatly solved, how beautiful the arrangement of a difficult problem on a page. That was the only time I ever heard her express an unfulfilled hope. She had been one of the first women to graduate from Stanford University and still wore her hair cut in a boyish bob, a style once considered a threat to home and family and country but now maintained in the interest of efficiency. Deep-set, lively blue eyes peered at the world with stubborn distrust. I think she was beautiful, the bones of her face cleaned of superfluous flesh, her aquiline nose stretching out and the nostrils flaring with each breath. She was like mathematics; a cipher, a code, a human being pared down to the essential parts. Nothing sloppy or sentimental about Miss Larson. She was ninety-six years old, a maiden lady without family and with few friends.

After she was forced to retire from teaching she moved into a private residence club and had lived there for thirty years. Her life was orderly — I was the first new variable, she said, in twenty years. She desired nothing, lacked nothing, did what she pleased in the order she pleased. She thought my life utter chaos, my politics anarchy, my appearance slovenly, my habits unhealthy. I thought her rigid, frozen, unemotional, detached; I once told her I thought I injected a bit of healthy dirt in her life. I was very fond of her and had no idea why she tolerated me.

She became ill during a bridge tournament. That morning, Miss Larson wakened early, excited and looking forward to a long day of playing her favorite game with first-rate opponents. She was conscious of mild nausea and a sharp pain in her side. But she was old and accustomed to functioning with occasional discomfort. Just excitement, she told herself as she carefully dressed. The thought of food made her feel even more nauseous, so she fixed a cup of tea in her room before going downstairs. The pain in her side was enough to make her move carefully and slowly. I am ninety-six years old, she thought, and I still get a catch in my side when I am excited. I remember my first day of teaching, it was the same thing. I couldn't eat, felt so weak, and those high school boys all looked so huge and menacing. Well, I soon showed them who ruled the classroom. And today, well, today I feel I am going to play fine bridge.

Miss Larson did play fine bridge, in spite of increasing pain in her side. She became very pale late in the afternoon and her partner was concerned. Everyone knew how old she was, and she had jokingly stated she would be happy to die playing bridge. By late afternoon her breathing was shallow and rapid. She was furious and refused to quit playing. She did play fine bridge that day, and when the final cards were played, she asked that someone call her doctor. She felt too faint to stand and the pain had become a grasping, digging presence, making breathing difficult. An ambulance was called, and she went directly from six hours of tournament bridge to the hospital operating room. Miss Larson had gallstones.

If one is young and reasonably healthy, having a gall bladder removed is still a major operation. If one also happens to be ninety-six years old, complications are expected.

In the case of Miss Larson, the operation was a complete success. No physical difficulties were experienced. She simply entered what she later referred to as her "psychedelic stage."

Three days after surgery, the night nurses were surprised to hear a loud, argumentative voice coming from her room. When they entered they found her standing by her bed, shaking her fist at a corner of the room and demanding that her pupils pay attention to the algebra lesson. She was confused when confronted by the nurses and began to cry. Throughout that night and early morning, the staff found it necessary to keep someone in the room. The next morning, the doctor ordered private duty nurses twenty-four hours a day for Miss Larson, and she became the first patient I had cared for in four years. She found this very amusing, during her lucid moments, because we had often argued about my reasons for disliking nursing and preferring to continue my education in other fields.

"I see things," she announced to me that first morning. "I think someone gave me some drug. At night, when the hospital is sound asleep, I wake and the room is filled with colors, with dimly remembered faces, with funny music. Sometimes I will find myself talking quite lucidly to someone who just isn't there, someone who died a long time ago. I feel one moment like I am five years old, and my father is holding me on his lap; or I am on a train and have cinders in my eyes. Last night I taught my first class all over again — and, oh, I didn't want to do it then or now. I argued with my father about going to graduate school. 'I must,' I told him. 'I can be a really great mathematician.' But as I was talking to him, his face became a rainbow and slid off down the wall and he disappeared. The nurses came in . . . if they've given me some drug, for experiments, they should tell me. It isn't fair, I shouldn't have to relive all that again. If every night for the rest of my life is going to be this way; if all my dreams are going to be distortions of the past, with time and color and everything all running together, I would just as soon die now. I can't do it all again, I can't be that strong all over again, not now. Not after all these years."

During the day she was fine, if tired and dozing most of the time. But when darkness came she entered a shadowy world, a world seen only by her. In hospitals they call it "sundowning" and it is a common thing with old people when they are removed from a familiar environment and placed in the hospital. The darkness, the lack of familiar things around them, the strange sounds from the corridors cause a sort of sensory confusion which brings on hallucinations. Usually the simple act of turning on a night light will chase away the shadows, and the old people will sleep. But in Miss Larson's case, a light was not enough. She had lived a very long time in her rooms at the residence club; she was rather rigid and didn't take well to change. Perhaps that is why she had such terrible night visitors. In any case, for ten days her nights were filled with horrors, and her days spent in exhausted, fitful dozing. These are not conditions in which to recover from major surgery, and her physical condition became steadily weaker. She ate little, found any physical activity, even passive exercise, exhausting, did not want visitors, would not, finally, even read the daily bridge column in the newspaper. She seemed well on her way to becoming a senile old lady.

I had much the easiest shift; the evening and night nurses found her impossible. "She is always asking me why I don't wear a white uniform, or why I dye my hair green, or what time is it, or what did I put in her water; and telling me to get out. There she is sitting upright in her bed, clutching the side rails, all eighty pounds and ninety-six years of her, screeching her head off that I'm some cheating schoolgirl. The woman's clearly batty, and I don't know how much longer I can take it. Besides, her insurance will cover only so much in the hospital, and so many days of private nursing, and then off she goes into a nursing home. She can't stay here, disturbing sick people and upsetting the nurses all night."

I would spend my days trying to keep Miss Larson awake and moving, so that she would sleep at night and not be "a bother." Coaxing, prodding, nagging, until she came to view even me as the enemy.

"You take drugs, don't you?" she accused one day. "You even think it's good experience, and expands the head or some such nonsense. Well, I am not taking anything from you, young lady. Someone is trying to drive me crazy, drive me into one of those awful homes for old people, where I'll die . . . Do you want that? Do you? Will you please tell me what is happening, what is wrong, what have they given me . . ."

Yes, she was very paranoid. And uncooperative. And becoming weaker. But the lucid moments became more frequent, and she began to beg to be taken home. The hospital was a malignant presence to her, a place filled with ghosts and sudden, unexplained noises in the night. She was, to my mind, coherent but unreasonable in her demands. She could barely stand, could not walk without help. She continued to be suspicious of all nurses, but she had always been suspicious. She was extremely demanding, even more so after she discovered the private duty nurses received forty dollars a shift. She expected to receive her money's worth. The night nurse quit after Miss Larson caught her dozing in a chair and threw a pitcher of water in that general direction.

The next morning her doctor announced that, due to her slow recovery and the general overcrowding in the hospital, she must consider moving to a convalescent hospital. Since she lived alone, she must be physically able to care for herself before discharge. Meals and maid service were available in the residence club, but no personal care. Now Miss Larson became really upset. She had friends who simply disappeared in such places; she believed people went there when there was no chance for recovery. "Death houses for the old," I heard her mutter. "I'll go to the street first." But it wasn't as if she really had a choice. The hospital needed her bed for acutely ill patients, and other facilities were available for long-term care.

The doctor informed the nursing staff and the hospital social worker that Miss Larson was to be transferred to an "extended care facility." He recommended several places in the vicinity, and the social worker came to talk to Miss Larson.

"Social worker." A strange title and an even stranger woman. Her job at this particular hospital consisted in finding places to send people who were no longer in need of intensive nursing care, who could not be helped by all the technology gathered in a modern hospital, who were, in short, no longer medically interesting or likely to improve drastically. The job was more like that of a travel agent, and the woman had even absorbed some of the impersonal, smiling manner of those thousands of clerks one encounters when trying to buy airline tickets. Miss Larson was convinced this woman was only selling one-way tickets, and was hostile and withdrawn.

"You're very lucky, Emily, my, you don't look ninety-six years old, we've found a perfectly lovely place just down the block from here, a new place run by perfectly lovely competent people recommended by your doctor. Everything will be taken care of before you leave here, I just need a few answers to some simple questions and you can be moved immediately, and doctor says you are to have a nurse with you for a few days until you get used to the change. Now, let me see, I can't get over your being so . . spry. This is a lovely new convalescent hospital, with a recreation worker, and a professional staff, and your doctor can see you there. Now, Emily, if you will just tell me your social security number . . . is she listening to me?"

"I think she turned off her hearing aid when you called her by her first name. She regards that as impertinent; she doesn't want to go to this place, and I don't blame her for being uncooperative," I answered. "If you need any information, it should be on her admission forms here. I think Miss Larson understands that she is being moved on orders from her doctor, and there isn't much we can do. But she doesn't feel any need to be polite."

"Doctor says . . ." The woman was only doing her job. I didn't want to be rude, but she showed no understanding of the crushing blow Miss Larson had received. For years, she had managed to avoid a nursing home, and now, through the benevolence of Medicare, she was eligible for, and forced to accept, institutionalization. There was no way the social worker could sugarcoat the pill, no family she could smile at and be helpful to, no gratitude from the withdrawn old lady in the bed.

This was a very determined social worker, however. She explained the process to me: Medicare provided for one hundred days of benefits in an extended care facility when a patient had spent at least three days in a hospital prior to admission, and was in need of skilled nursing treatment and rehabilitation for the same illness for which admission to a hospital had been necessary. In 1966, when Medicare benefits became available, few extended care facilities were available. Minimal federal standards of quality were expected — proper dietary supervision, twenty-four hours of personalized nursing service, a clean and safe physical plant geared to rehabilitation and comfort — but most nursing homes could not meet these standards. Federal funds were available, however, for enterprising builders to construct new facilities. The home to which Miss Larson was to be transported had been built as one of a chain on such guaranteed loans. A miracle of social welfare; someone receives money to build special places to take care of people no one knows what to do with; is guaranteed payment from the government for at least part of the care, the first one hundred days anyway; and after that the patient could be readmitted to a general hospital for three days, and back to the extended care facility; the whole thing more profitable than running a hotel because you charge more whenever "medical" enters the picture, and the overhead is not so much more . . . very enterprising. Small wonder that large motel and hotel chains were the first to move into this new business.

First impressions of Montcliffe Convalescent Hospital were favorable. It was small, just thirty-six patients, and fairly new. The design and decoration of the building was modern California motel; long and low, with large expanses of glass covered by serviceable beige drapes. Every floor was carpeted and walls were newly painted beige. Large and fantastically colored sprays of plastic flowers dominated every flat surface and each room had sliding glass doors opening into a narrow walk surrounding the building. The place was unimaginative, impersonal, tasteless, but not anything really objectionable. It was simply ugly. Everything was covered in plastic; even the lampshades and chairs shone with pristine plastic newness, untouched by human hands. All in all, it looked like the sort of motel, moderately priced, favored by salesmen because they all look alike and thus come to be homey. A place for transients.

Miss Larson and I were directed to a four-bed room; no, they didn't have space available in a two-bed room; yes, they knew it was requested and as

soon as space was available . . . please just fill out
these forms, sign this release, list all valuables, you
know how it is when you are old, you forget what
you had. Yes, that is your bed, honey, right by the
door, and you can keep your things in the stand right
there, nothing on top, please, it looks so messy when
one clutters up the tops of things. Just tuck it all
away, that's right. Now, dearie, you just rest and the
nurse and I will take care of everything . . .

The woman in charge of the Montcliffe Convalescent Hospital was a registered nurse. She was required by law, a fixture like firedoors or ramps; new
to her job, frightened of old people, and with a tend-
ency to avoid looking you in the eye. She bustled,
chirped, patted, pulled, and quickly disappeared. All
of the actual patient care was done by the "aides" or
"attendants." They are not trained to do their jobs,
and they learn by watching other attendants. Their
skill and interest depend a good deal on whom they
work with the first days. Some are good, some terrible. All are underpaid. It's a job, a job for the un-
skilled, for women with children to support and no
hope in their future; for women whose legs are already swollen and tired from thankless day labor in a
million other jobs like this one; they must work, and
it's a job.

The room was not unpleasant but very uncomfortable. Four beds, precision-lined against one wall, faced a blank beige wall on the other side. Four nightstands, flush against the beds. One chair in the corner. A vague smell, like urine and green soap mixed and used to wash the floors. No color, only beige walls, beige drapes, beige floor, white covers on the beds. Three beds were occupied, two by silent unmoving figures, looking as if a child had placed pillows under the sheets to fool his parents, and the bed nearest Miss Larson's (I already thought of it as "her" spot; she simply sat in the wheelchair, head down, hearing aid off, hands moving restlessly in her lap) was completely filled by an extremely obese — grayly fat, no pink skin, just mounds of bulging, unfeeling flesh — woman, who moved constantly, her lips pulling in and out like a baby waiting to be fed.

It was nearly four o'clock, time for me to be leaving. I wanted out of that place very badly. It was all so clean, so neat, but underneath it felt just like the "Old Folks Home" in Douglas. The smell, the ambience were alike; only the surface was different. We have certainly improved care of the aged in all those highly visible ways like clean linen, modern buildings, professional staff, even fire regulations. The package has been sanitized, wrapped in plastic, and labeled fit for public funding. But it felt the same, and I didn't want to leave Miss Larson in that place.

However, I smiled a very professional nurse-y smile, efficiently tucked her in bed without letting myself feel compassion, and thought that the doctor *must* know best, after all, he is the doctor, and refused to meet Miss Larson's miserable, half-uttered pleas that I not leave her alone. I went home, and by morning convinced myself the place wasn't so bad, that I was simply against institutions without really giving any particular place a chance to be different, and resolved that I would do my best to make Miss Larson's stay comfortable, easy, and as short as possible.

The first morning began with a lecture by the charge nurse. I must help Miss Larson adjust to being in Montcliffe and help her understand that she was not different, that it was very unusual for people to have private nurses in the home, and that a certain routine must be observed in order to encourage independence and rehabilitation. As she talked, I could see the aides pushing patients in wheelchairs out of their rooms and into the hall. Under thin cotton bath blankets, the old people were naked. Some were confused, pulling the cloth off their wrinkled flesh, mouths and hands constantly working, sometimes uttering small wordless cries. Others sat miserably hunched in their chairs and held the thin blankets tightly around bent shoulders. Someone had pulled Miss Larson out of bed and she was sitting in the

line, looking around wildly, her neck rigid with in-
dignation. "No, no, I have a nurse, no, no . . ." I
could hear her protest.

"Oh, it's bath time for those on the north hall," said
the charge nurse. "We give baths twice a week,
showers, actually, so much more refreshing, don't
you think? And we change the linen, all the linen, at
the same time. Old people sometimes don't like to
bathe, you know, so we keep them on a very clean
schedule. Why, some of them never even move from
bed except on bath days."

I could hear Miss Larson. "No, no, I can bathe myself, just let me alone, I can do it." Some of the other
patients were looking at her, without interest and
without pity. We all have to do it, they seemed to be
saying. Don't fight it. No distinctions. What makes
you think you're so different. Men, women, confused,
coherent, all the same. To the showers!

Two aides, one on each side, would pick up the old
carcasses, place them in a molded plastic shower
chair, deftly remove the blanket, push them under
the shower and rather haphazardly soap them down.
A few minutes for rinsing, a quick rubdown with an
already damp towel, back under the blanket and
ready for the next. The aides were quick, efficient,
not at all brutal; they kept up a running conversation
between themselves about food prices, the new shoes

one had bought, California divorce laws. They might have been two sisters doing dishes. Lift, scrub, rinse, dry, put away. Lift, scrub, rinse, dry, put away. And did you hear the one about . . .

I gave Miss Larson a bath in her room that morning, over the strenuous objections of the charge nurse, who felt I was encouraging separation and dependence. I felt guilty, and my hands were unnecessarily rough as I turned and bathed Miss Larson. It was as if I blamed her for placing me in a position where I had to be miserable, observe misery. How could she do it to me?

The resentment I felt so strongly that first morning seems endemic in places where the aged live. The custodians, whether medically trained or administrative, always seem to have some anger, some residual hatred or fear of their charges. Sometimes I felt it was fear of one's own aging process, or just anger at having to do a very difficult job. Sometimes I saw it as a sort of natural turning away from another's misery, the way one will ignore the open trousers of an old man on the subway. But even if it was a sense of delicacy, of not wanting to intrude on the last years these old people had on earth, it soon progressed to another level. Because the attendants had to physically care for, handle the aging bodies of these old people, they began to treat them as if they were infants, unhearing, uncaring, unable to speak or communicate in any way. The patients were uniformly called honey or dearie or sweetie — or sometimes naughty girl if they soiled their beds — just as one tends to call children by pet names. At that level, the attendants expected gratitude or at least silent acquiescence from the old people and their families. The bodies were kept clean, fed, powdered, combed, and clothed. They were as infants, without modesty or sex or privacy.

The next level involved treating the patients as inanimate objects rather than as any kind of human being, adult or infant. This attitude was most frequent in older staff members and is understandably defensive. "Ahhh, she's *just* an old lady," they would say. "She's *just* an old lady." And that seemed to justify all manner of things, including the way blind patients were fed or not fed, according to whim; or how soon an old man was cleaned and his linen changed after he soiled his bed.

And Montcliffe Convalescent Hospital is a *good* hospital. It is expensive, and the bills are occasionally padded. For example, a patient who required linen changes more than twice a week was charged extra; most of these old people lost control of their bowels or bladder frequently, if only because the attendants were not particularly prompt to answer bells. Patients who could not feed themselves were charged a dollar per meal for the service. Drugs were ordered from a local pharmacy, and the pharmacist told me he paid a regular fee for the privilege of providing medication to this particular chain of extended care facilities. Doctors charged the patients for regular visits, even if the visit consisted of a two minute how-do from the doorway.

These are all frequent infractions in these types of facilities; you read about them every day. The passage of the Medicare Act does provide better care for some old people; it also lines the pockets and provides better retirement plans for others.

Besides the nursing care program (baths twice a week, enemas when required, tranquilizers and sleeping pills as directed, part of each day spent out of bed, etc.) Montcliffe also boasted a part-time recreation therapist. She hadn't been trained for her job, but she had the disposition and character. Nothing depressed her and she seemed oblivious to the depression around her. Surrounded by "her girls," who were all nodding and fidgeting in wheelchairs and who had not uttered a sound, she would chirp "Oh, this is such fun, isn't it girls? We must do this [watch television, play bingo, clap hands, whatever] more often!"

Miss Smiles loved programs. If you ever wonder

what happens to all the kids you knew in junior high school who played the accordion, or did acrobatic dancing, or recited illuminating poetry; if you ever wonder what an earnest but amateur photographer does with all his colored slides of the Holy Land, the pyramids, the Changing of the Guard; if you wonder where ladies go to do good works these days; let me tell you: they impose themselves on the aged. During the first week at the Montcliffe facility, we had two lectures, with slides, given by local ministers, one lady (in costume) who played the dulcimer and sang songs in an uncertain soprano, and a demonstration of flower arranging. The contrast between the formal, mannered Japanese flower arrangements and the riotous obscenities of the plastic sprays around the room was fairly hilarious. Unfortunately, the lady giving the demonstration had no sense of humor or any other kind of sense; to show arrangements of funeral sprays in a house of the dying shows little sensitivity.

These programs took place in what Miss Larson and I began calling "the parking lot." This was a large room, beige brightened by a touch of bright orange, designated the recreation room by Miss Smiles. Most of the day it was filled with old people — pushed in wheelchairs and left to doze in long lines against the wall, or pulled by the hand of an impatient aide, tottering in to sit in one of the low, plastic chairs. The chairs seemed expressly designed for the discomfort of old bones; they were too low for the aged to move in and out of without help; they were covered with slick plastic which meant they were cold to the touch in winter and sticky in the summer; and they were hard. Miss Larson refused to patronize the "parking lot"; she said the sight of that many old bodies lined up waiting for the undertaker depressed her. No communication ever seemed to take place between patients; no conversation ever took place in the parking lot. The only people who spoke were those whose job it was to entertain. When no program was scheduled, a large color television set was turned on. The patients were not to touch the set, and it was frequently out of focus. Evidently one old man had, during the last baseball season, become so angry at the television set or his team's bad performance, or the refusal of an aide to change the station, that he had kicked the set. Now there was a small polite sign asking that no one touch the set. The old man, it seemed, was no longer with us, and the television set still refused to work.

I often wondered why there was barely any conversation among the patients. They weren't all senile; Montcliffe had a policy against admitting "vegetable cases." Some even seemed anxious to talk, but spoke only to the aides or an occasional visitor. They simply didn't talk among themselves and even avoided looking at each other. Those who weren't bedridden ate in a common dining room, yet meals were silent, hurried affairs, filled only with the scraping of spoons and the occasional click of slipping dentures. It was true the aides rushed the meals, because they ate after the tables were cleared and everyone was back in the parking lot. But I don't think anyone ever said as much as "pass the salt" or "lovely day today." Among themselves they remained almost mute.

Why? I had thought that one pleasure left to the aged was the time to chat, to share experiences, to tell and retell favorite stories. This wasn't true at Montcliffe. Why? The reasons were curious and subtle and cruel. For one thing, the staff assumed that any and all remarks were addressed to them, since these old people couldn't possibly have anything to say. If Mrs. X said, "Lovely day today," to her roommate, Mrs. Y, to give one example, Aide Johnson would answer, "Is the sun in your eyes, dearie? Do you want the curtains closed?" And effectively, slowly, Mrs. X would learn that only the aides had the power of speech.

I think the staff regarded conversation between patients as silly and meaningless, because they believed the patients incapable of thought. But something else was going on: it was as if two patients talking would be a dangerous thing. I saw, on more than one occasion, patients arbitrarily separated in the middle of a quiet chat. I observed two old women, moved, perhaps, by a dim memory of time spent with friends long ago, begin to talk as they waited to have their hair done. One of them was suddenly told she would have to wait until next week and wheeled, still in midsentence, to her room. There was no apparent malice in the aide's action; she seemed to be enforcing some unwritten rule, responding to an institutional credo that said patients mustn't chat.

Miss Larson entered Montcliffe the last week in October. The air was cool and fresh and in the sun it was quite warm, so we spent a good part of our day outside. I was becoming increasingly impatient with her; her condition was deteriorating in spite of all my efforts. No matter what I did she simply refused to get better. I blamed her for imposing her weakness on me; but whenever she became too demanding, I would just walk away and have a cigarette in the dining room. Shortly after her admission, I arrived at 7 A.M. to find the night nurse indignant and angry. Miss Larson had climbed over the side rails during the night, and had been found in the bathroom. "She didn't ring or call out," said the nurse. "Her room is right opposite the desk, and I would have heard her. Why, she might have been hurt, and she is so confused. I want the doctor to order more sedation. We can't have her carrying on, and disturbing all the other patients. Finally, we had to put her in restraints and I repeated her sleeping pill. But she kept yelling all the same."

I walked in the room and Miss Larson was indeed in restraints; the look on her face was so angry, it seemed to me someone had tied her up in order to prevent murder. "Get me out of these!" she ordered. "How dare they try and stop me from getting out of bed. I always have to relieve myself at night; and they never answer my bell. Usually they come and hide the cord so I can't even find it. So I crawl over the edge; I've been doing it ever since I came to this place. Now you get me out of these, and tell that doctor I want to see him!"

Miss Larson was not confused; but in a place where all the patients are so sedated that they scarcely move a muscle during the night, she was counted a nuisance. I didn't want them to increase her sedation; barbiturates frequently make old people confused and disoriented. Even if she was a pain in the neck, I liked her better awake and making some sense. The problem was she had no rights. She was old, sick, feeble. Therefore she must shut up, lie still, take what little was offered and be grateful. And if she did that, she would be a "good girl."

There she was, ninety-six years old and didn't even know she was dependent on society. She thought her thirty years of teaching, her careful hoarding of the little she inherited from her family, and the benevolence of the Social Security Act, with amendments, would guarantee humane treatment in her old age. "You get what you pay for," she told me, "and I want a nurse here, at least during the day, until I'm strong enough to manage on my own. I don't want to depend on those" — with a scornful jerk of her head — "people for anything. I'll pay for your services, but I'm asking as a friend. Don't leave me alone with them. They just want to keep everyone in the parking lot until it's over."

I didn't want to leave her alone, and certainly understood her fears. The place was driving me crazy. I would catch myself sitting and staring at the wall with a vacant smile, my hands folded in my lap, just like one of the old people in the parking lot. I found myself ignoring the calls for help that came from rooms other than Miss Larson's because the aides had become so hostile to my "interference." The charge nurse gave me daily lectures on my letting Miss Larson become too dependent, how bad it was for her to get everything she wanted, how demanding she was to the other nurses, poor things. From the outside, Montcliffe Convalescent Hospital looked less like a modern motel and more like a bunker, a concrete dwelling hunching close to the ground, hiding secrets inside. The very air seemed menacing, full of deodorant sprays and powders and soaps and lint from the clothes dryer in the back hall; but underneath that smell, the smell of hidden decay, of urine and dying flesh, still was there, still assaulting the nose every morning at seven o'clock.

She was my friend and I wanted her well, healthy, back at the bridge table. But I couldn't stay with her forever. I became impatient, even angry, sometimes rough. I could feel a great distance between us — I was young, she was old — that had never existed on the outside. The hostility of them, the others, those people who worked in the hospital, was beginning to permeate the relationship we had. I began to really dislike Miss Larson. And we had been friends.

Miss Larson understood the stakes long before I did. It was a battle for her soul, a fight for her mind, with her weakened physical condition the trump card. Either she could give up, and wheel into the parking lot, or she could keep fighting and have everybody hate her, receive extra sedation to keep her mouth shut, be placed on mind-fogging tranquilizers to stop her demands. She had finally been moved to a two-bed room, out of the "nursery," as she called that original four-bed room, and her roommate was a quiet and rather sweet old lady. Miss Larson, unfortunately, had displaced a woman who had been in that bed for three years and who had been sent to the "nursery" over thin, weak little protests by both women. So Mrs. Gladstone retreated miserably into a shell, apparently determined never to get close to another human being for fear of losing them. Mrs. Lewis could be heard crying just two hundred feet away, but neither woman made any effort to move. Friendships were dangerous, hurtful things in Montcliffe. It wasn't death that hurt so much; it was unexpected, arbitrary deprivation. The staff had such incredible power over the minds and bodies of the old people in their care.

Halloween came. Miss Larson and I had come to an agreement; I would stay a few more days, then come back only for a few hours in the morning to help her bathe and dress. I explained to her I was interested in seeing other places where old people lived and had accepted a temporary job as a visiting nurse in order to do some quiet investigation. She had just glanced at me sharply, snorted unbelievingly, and turned off her hearing aid. I left the room to smoke a cigarette. She refused to listen, I refused to stay.

As I hurried down the hall to the dining room, I could hear Miss Smiles tittering away, pretending joy, fulfilling Montcliffe's promise for a balanced and interesting program of activities geared to the interest and rehabilitation of the old people in their care. It was Halloween, and the afternoon's activity was to be a party. "I ought to make the old lady go," I thought. "A Halloween party would really set her off!" The cook had prepared cupcakes decorated with tiny candy pumpkins, and apple cider in juice glasses. Miss Smiles, in her untidy blue smock, had been racing around all morning, trailing black and orange streamers. Every patient, with the exception of Miss Larson and an old man who said he was dying that day, was wheeled or pushed into the "parking lot" to attend the party.

Halloween. Hallowed Eve, the day before All Saints Day, the day that unfulfilled souls walk the earth and demand satisfaction. The door to the parking lot was filled with flickering light; they must have candles, I thought. I stopped outside the door and glanced in.

Smiles had outdone herself. Thirty-four old men and women sat lined up in the semidarkness, unmoving and quiet. One would give a phlegmy cough, another would clear her throat; hands picked at blankets or grasped the arms of the chairs tightly to prevent the tremors. The room was decorated as for a first grader's dreams of Halloween; all orange and black and skeletons dangling from the ceiling. Plastic pumpkins held flickering candles. No games were being played, no one spoke or moved, except Miss Smiles, who was fluttering about, "Oh, what fun, what fun! Are you excited, darling? Isn't this just lovely? We really must have parties more often!" I watched her move about, stopping before each one of the old people and moving her hands about their faces as if to evoke a spell, a running stream of words following her around the room. I had thought her an incredibly stupid woman, unimaginative and insensitive; but from the doorway, on this day, in her dark dress, she looked somehow sinister and evil. Suddenly she stopped her fluttery movements and stepped back, brushing her hands together briskly as if she had completed a hard and dusty task. "There!" she said. "Finished. Isn't it wonderful?" And she turned toward me, and flicked on the light. Then I could see what she had been doing. The faces of the old people were covered with masks, with crudely drawn skulls, garish pumpkins, little elves, evil witches. The old gray heads halved by tight elastic turned toward the door slowly as if all the masks were attached to one string and Miss Smiles had pulled them in my direction. There they were, drooling, twitching; some able to think coherently, some senile; women; men; private and charity cases; all distinctions gone, they joined the living dead. Witches, goblins, ghosts, skeletons, twisted bodies topped by a child's nightmare of faces. I backed out of the room, one hand lifted to ward off some imagined evil, some vision of my own future, locked in a world like this, forced to attend meaningless functions, eat tasteless food, live friendless, penniless, sour and old; was that the future? "No," I thought. "No, I don't want to get old."

Eleven

DISTANCES are no longer measured in miles; we have developed a way of measuring by the amount of time it takes to get there. I flew over the Sierras, the Great American Desert, the Rocky Mountains; had a brief moment over the Great Plains and the smaller, gentler Appalachian Mountains, and entered the northeastern United States. When the plane landed in New York City I had only the vaguest sense of how huge this country is. The West was divided into two cocktails and dinner, the Midwest was coffee and a movie, and before I had time for a nap we were landing at Kennedy Airport. There was four hours' distance between one way of life and another.

I had come to the city to escape from the draining, dragging lethargy left by old battle wounds. I felt a little bit like a caricature of "small town girl escapes to big city," but with the help of friends I soon developed some of the superficial characteristics of the city dweller. Those first few weeks remain hazy, full of time spent on subways, buses, on foot; learning to ignore little tragedies on the street and being mugged twice; and trying to find an apartment and a job. I had never lived in a real city. I found New Yorkers beautiful. I walked the streets and stared into closed, harried faces; saw models from magazine pages running from one appointment to another, mingling with drunks and pushcart operators; all of them looking so wise and so touched by life; every bone and piece of flesh molded and formed by life in the city. Every moment my eye was delighted by another memorable face, caught by a glimpse of another way of being. I fell in love with New York. I went to the top of the Empire State Building, on the Staten Island Ferry, to all the museums, walked in Central Park, visited the Bronx Zoo, saw an off-Broadway play that was raided by the police. And when someone asked *me* for directions, I knew I was a New Yorker.

I found a job easily enough. Every city has a short-age of nurses, and even though I didn't want a straight nursing job, I went to work at a state mental hospital. The thought was depressing, the hospital it-self even more so. Before I went inside the door I thought the architect had been possessed by some idea of prisons and cardboard cartons and mauso-leums as he sat at his drawing board. Or maybe the building had not been designed at all; maybe institu-tions now come prefabricated, marked "multi-purpose custodial care building, suitable for mad-house, prison, or boarding school."

The job was working at a large New York State mental hospital, but not within the hospital itself. I was a member of a team whose concern was to pre-vent admissions to the hospital. Our methods were pretty unorthodox and we were pretty successful. What would happen is this: Someone would be brought to the psychiatric emergency room at a nearby city hospital, either by friends, family or po-lice, and would be diagnosed as "psychotic" by the doctor. Instead of admitting the person to the hospi-tal, the doctor would refer the patient to our team, and we would work with the patient, his family, his neighbors, the police, the schools; try, in fact, to pre-vent the necessity for admission to a hospital. We would try and create some sort of space for a person labeled as mentally disturbed to work through problems without having to suffer the stigma of admission to a state mental hospital. We knew we couldn't "cure" any deep-seated psychoses, but we could help people return to some pre-crisis level of functioning. Then, with support and help from other agencies, and sometimes out-patient therapy, people had a chance to live a fairly normal life without hospitalization.

That was our job. The team was working against long-established practice; almost anyone who comes into a psychiatric emergency room, whose behavior is the slightest bit strange or who seems to be an "interesting" case, is admitted to the hospital. The hospital exists to shelter people, not to encourage them to continue living in their communities. It also exists as a teaching institution, and budding doctors need interesting cases to learn from.

The busiest hours of the psychiatric emergency room are the night hours, holidays, periods of bad weather. People get uneasy, nightmares become real, families get tired of listening to Uncle Harry breaking the furniture in his room. All the bad dreams of the city seem to rise and walk and find their way down to city hospital. The room is too small and crowded, hot in summer and too cold in the winter. People weep, laugh, mumble and scream; a man in the corner sits and stares at his hands, turning them over and over, examining them carefully for the mark of some unknown crime. A young girl sits quietly, looking fresh and pretty, slowly and methodically ripping her dress until she is surrounded by bits of thread. Two policemen stand by a man strapped on a stretcher, his body taut as a bowstring, his hands clenched into white fists.

This is where people come when there is no place else; when the priest, the lady upstairs, the corner grocer, the police, the community can no longer tolerate their behavior. They come for help.

I came to my new job like someone who had just discovered suffering and was determined to cure it all.

The old were especially neglected, I noticed. They would be the last called to see the doctor, because their craziness was the quiet, polite madness of the aged. They were depressed, usually, not violent or dangerous. Old men in the city, particularly, seem prone to suicide. Usually they are successful, but sometimes someone finds them and brings them into the emergency room. Old women sometimes forget to eat or sleep and sit for longer and longer periods of time in their chairs, drifting back in time, remembering how things were, trying to forget what it means to be old and alone and afraid. And sometimes someone remembers they are there, and calls the police to come and carry the cold, half-dead body to the emergency room. Families would notice that Aunt Mabel has been hoarding food in her room again, and talking about the great famine she is going to bring unto the unjust, and when they get tired of listening to her rambling, incoherent voice they bring her into the emergency room. Do something, doctor, she — they — he — is driving us crazy.

As psychiatric cases, the old were not considered too interesting. They were, both to the psychiatrist and to the community, more of a problem in disposal. Most old people don't belong in the mental hospital, but where else can they go? What can a young psychiatrist, confronted with a seventy-year-old woman who calls him by the name of a long-dead husband, what can that doctor do? She's not really acutely ill, not really crazy; she is confused, doesn't know who the President is or what day of the week it is. She is too old to think in terms of curing her symptoms, vague as they are. Our team would try and find family, friends, some sort of community support network to enable the old lady to stay in her own little hole; but we couldn't always find anyone to help.

When the team would receive a referral from the emergency room, I found my eyes would quickly skip to where the age was given. If the person was over fifty, even, sometimes, over forty, I would feel the beginnings of despair. It was so difficult to get anyone interested, to find anyone to care, about people who were "past their prime." Another old loner, I would think. And I knew how they lived, in a tiny cluttered apartment or a dingy hotel room, not eating properly because the money was short; doing without food to buy tobacco or wine. If only they would take care of themselves, I thought, then they wouldn't have been noticed. Then they could have lived out their days without interference. But they didn't always care about living, with loneliness their only companion and only voices from the past to fill the silent rooms.

I remember one old man, Charlie, brought in by a screaming, hurrying ambulance. His neighbors smelled gas, called the police, and when the door was broken in they found him with his head in the oven. No note, he had no one to write to, no one who would care. He was only fifty-five. Quick, efficient, impersonal resuscitation brought him around. The doctor called our team. When Charlie was able to sit up, I was standing by the bed. He didn't ask where he was, he knew; he had been in the emergency room the week before, saying he was depressed, felt he was dying, needed help. He was given some antidepressant pills, a few brisk words of advice, and sent home.

When Charlie opened his eyes and glanced around

the room, he just sighed. "Well, not this time," he said. "But a man has a right to die, don't he? He don't have to just sit and wait, sit and wait for death? Why don't you just let me alone?"

I didn't have any answer for Charlie. He was sent home again, with more pills, and a stern lecture about endangering other people by turning on the gas. I tried to get him interested in visiting senior citizen centers in his area, in finding some kind of parttime work he could do, in trying to reestablish contact with his family. He was grateful, polite, and seemed to listen. But I felt his mind was made up, that he was through, finished, just didn't want to be bothered. He wanted me out of the way; he didn't want to embarrass me by doing anything while I was around, but his eyes had an empty, waiting look, as if he was listening to a call I couldn't hear. One day he told me he was moving out of the district, and wouldn't be seeing me again.

"You don't have to move, Charlie. I'll stop bothering you. Honest. I mean, you've lived here a long time, it would be hard for you to find a place . . ." I stopped, I couldn't say that I understood, that he had a right to kill himself and I had nothing real to offer that could make him want to live. How could I fill the empty cup? He had been alone a long time. He knew what he was doing, he just didn't want to live.

No psychiatrist could help him find the interest in life, no pills could make him believe there was anything he wanted to do. He lived in a closet on the fringe of a great city, and found no way to be a part of the human community. Age had simply magnified his problems; he didn't want to be *kept* alive, he wanted to at least have that choice. I left, and we didn't say good-bye.

Once we were called to a home because the lady of the house, a woman of sixty-eight, had suddenly taken it into her head to destroy all the furniture. She had done a pretty good job by the time we arrived, and pieces of tables, lamps, mirrors, three broken dining chairs, and dishes were piled neatly in the middle of the living room. When her husband stopped her destruction, she had simply fallen asleep on the couch, stating her intention never to move again. That had been some twenty-four hours before our arrival, and she was keeping her promise.

The team walked in and began to clear away the debris. The husband had been afraid to move anything; he had spent the time watching his wife sleep. After we had things cleared away, I tried talking to the old lady, but, although I knew she had watched us clean the room, she would not respond. Every time I asked her a question, the husband would answer. Finally, one member of the team brought in a coffee cake and asked the husband if we could make some coffee. He jumped up from his chair, looking confused, and stuttered, "Well, I don't know, I never make . . ."

The old lady got up from the couch, saying, "He doesn't know beans about a kitchen. I'll make coffee." And we spent an enjoyable hour over coffee and cake, although she refused to tell us why she had torn the house up. We would go back every week or so and have coffee; she never had any more trouble. I don't know what happened, or why she stopped. But she seemed to function after that one episode of mad energy. Her husband suggested that maybe she was just tired of furniture.

I had no formal psychiatric training, but I could feel that psychiatrists, as a rule, had little or no interest in the old. Formal psychoanalysis is useless with the aged; sudden dramatic cures infrequent. The excuse is always available that any problem of aberrant behavior in someone over sixty is the result of irreversible brain damage. "Organic," said the white coats, shaking their heads slowly. So most of the old people we saw were regarded as hopeless cases, disposal problems, merely a question of finding the proper custodial care.

But no one really knows if that is true. You can teach an old dog new tricks, I thought. Rehabilitation is possible, even if there is brain damage. I just didn't know enough, no one cared enough, there wasn't time enough; the priorities lie with the young, the known curables. I found myself beginning to turn away, to look away, as old people shuffled through the waiting room on their way to the back wards of one state mental hospital or another. What could I do? Everyone said they couldn't be helped. Good-bye, Charlie. . . .

In old age the frequency of mental illness reaches its peak, and as the number of elderly persons in the population increases, the seriousness of the problem for society also increases. The actual relationship of aging to mental illness can only be guessed at; doctors vary in diagnostic ability and the criteria used to assess psychiatric conditions. What is "normal" behavior in one person may be "neurotic" in another. We accept eccentricities in behavior, dress, habits, in teen-agers that we would regard as weird in our parents. Certain occupations allow more room for variety — artists, musicians — than others — doctors, lawyers — and our standards for judging people include these factors as well as age. But the older you are, the more likely the psychiatrist is to regard any abnormal behavior as part of "old age."

Theoretically, the practice in psychiatry is to distinguish two broad categories of mental disorders: functional and organic. An organic ailment can be traced, directly or indirectly, to some disease, injury or malfunction in the brain. This could be a tumor, cardiovascular defects, or drugs or poisons including alcohol. Functional ailments are those which arise where no definite malfunction can be detected, and where socially unacceptable patterns of behavior such as phobias or paranoid ideas are acquired.

Symptom patterns vary widely according to the kind of personality the patient had before the onset of the "disease"; furthermore, degenerative changes in the brain observed during autopsy (such as thickening and hardening of the blood vessels, the loss of many nerve cells, wider and deeper convolutions of the brain tissue) occur both in the brains of "normal" old people and people who had severe psychotic disorders. This may mean that some people can tolerate a degree of degenerative change in the brain, just as they adjust to defects in their aging bodies.

Perhaps it is more realistic to discuss mental illness in old age empirically: How and why do old people become labeled "mentally ill"? Why do they end up locked in mental hospitals?

It may sound cynical, or even flippant, but I think the answer is simply this: When someone's behavior begins to bother someone else, it comes to the attention of private or public social agencies involved in categorizing people as normal or abnormal. Every day, on the streets of the city, you see people you *know* are psychotic. Their behavior is somehow demented, offensive, strange, crazy. Yet they may function quite well, and are able to eat, work, find a bed, dress, amuse themselves. If examined by a psychiatrist they would be labeled "schizophrenic" or suffering from "senile dementia." It is a difficult judgment to make, both for society and for the doctor, but somehow, I always feel the aged are better off in familiar environments than strange, crowded hospitals.

There are some organic disorders, such as cerebral arteriosclerosis, syphilitic infection, and the excessive prolonged use of alcohol, which gradually cause erosion of memory, impaired judgment, and the loss of normal patterns of behavior. These disorders are usually irreversible. Supportive medical measures and custodial care are the only things we have to offer.

But many of the "affective" disorders which cause people — or their families — to seek psychiatric care *are* reversible. The individual may not be able to deal appropriately and realistically with his environment; his relationships with other people are impaired; and his thoughts may be bizarre — even paranoid — and his actions disorganized. He may be depressed, anxious, have psychosomatic complaints, even be confused. Right now, all we have to offer older people suffering from these disorders is supportive medical measures and, perhaps, custodial care.

The alternatives are rather limited, it seems. There is one other: The rate of suicide among old people is high. Social isolation, loss of status, inactivity, poverty; all contribute to the fact that suicide is a major cause of death among the aged.

The Gruner family had spent three days in the psychiatric emergency room of City Hospital. Father, mother, and daughter sat stoically, feet flat on the floor, untouched by the little mad bits of drama around them. Mr. Gruner was eighty-one, strong-featured and rather handsome, with iron-gray hair and a fine broad forehead. From the chin down he was withered and emaciated; I wondered where he got the energy to continue the rolling, jerking motions of Parkinson's disease. His hands were in constant motion, pill-rolling, drawing against his chest, back to his knees; he occasionally jostled the arm of his wife. She sat quietly most of the time, looking like she was still waiting on Ellis Island. Every half hour or so, she would jump up and begin shouting incomprehensible sentences, punctuated by throwing her hands in the air in an appeal to God. No one could understand her, she seemed to be speaking a combination of Yiddish and gibberish; yet everyone knew she was complaining. Her voice was the voice of all our aged grandparents: You never come to see me, you don't eat right, you're too thin, when are you going to get married and settled down?

Most of Mrs. Gruner's complaints seemed to be directed at the daughter, Anna, who sat a little apart from her parents and turned angrily away whenever anyone tried to speak to her. She had terrible acne, the kind that leaves your skin raw and red between pustules. The large nose, noble on her father, stuck out between her diseased cheeks like the beak of a sad parrot. Anna had been born late in her parents' life. She had been shy and alone, partly because of the acne, partly because she was raised by aging parents who understood little what a girl wanted or dreamed about. It was understood by her that she was brought into the world for one purpose: to take care of her parents. She had worked as a bookkeeper for a few years, but when her father began to have trouble getting around because of the Parkinson's disease, she quit to stay home and help her mother. The family had always been a tight, self-sufficient unit; her mother was suspicious of strangers and did not encourage friendships. Anna never had a friend. She had been raised to do her duty, and her duty was

her parents. This new trouble, this being thrown out
of their home, was more than she could manage. She
felt she had failed her parents, had failed to protect
them from danger. So she sat, guilty and despairing,
not hearing her mother's shouts, but only that inner
voice saying, you failed, you failed, it's all your fault,
you did it, you failed.

The family had been brought to the psychiatric
emergency room by the police. They had barricaded
the door against a city marshal who had come to
evict them from their home. The patrolmen were
called and finally had to break down the door of the
apartment. One policeman was treated for deep
scratches on his face, inflicted by Anna when he tried
to carry her from the apartment. The Gruners had
occupied that apartment for thirty years.

The police report said that the condition of the
apartment was enough to turn your stomach. Most of
the windows were broken and repaired with pieces of
cardboard; the walls bore evidence of furious family
fights. Neighbors reported that for three years the
family seldom left the building, having their gro-
ceries delivered and leaving their garbage in the halls
for other tenants to remove. Mrs. Gruner's brother visited occasionally, but for the last few months, the
family would not see him.

The family had little in the way of possessions;

most of the furniture was broken, old, useless. The
city marshal reported that it was barely worth the
effort it took to carry things down four flights of
stairs. Exactly what happened to it then was anybody's guess; since the Gruners had been taken away
by the police, their few possessions had probably
been taken by scavengers. The family was left with
nothing but the clothes they wore.

The police did not want to arrest the family, even
though they could be charged with assault. Since the
combined weight of all three Gruners barely equaled
that of one New York City patrolman, embarrassment motivated mercy, and the officers decided the
whole family was crazy enough to be locked up in an
institution. The patrol car brought the family to the
emergency room and no one there knew what to do
with them. The social worker on duty sent the family
to a "Welfare Hotel" downtown; the family refused to
stay there. One of the attendants on duty knew of an
apartment available; the family refused to stay there,
stating that they wanted only to go home. For three
days the staff of the emergency room tried to find a
home, a roof, a member of their family, someplace,
anyplace. The Gruners refused to move. The old lady
kept getting crazier and crazier; now she wasn't even
speaking Yiddish, but just jumping up and screaming
now and then. Anna was sullen and withdrawn, re-

fusing to speak. Mr. Gruner just sat, that beautiful
old head perched on top of the physical ruin, shaking
and jerking more than ever.

So it went for four days. The police brought them
in early Friday morning, and on Tuesday they still
sat in the emergency room. Here was a family,
thrown out of their home, all possessions lost, all
nightmares realized; and they sat in a row like they
were waiting for a train to come and take them away.
They ate cookies and sodas from the vending ma-
chines; they shook and mumbled and stared; they
smelled.

No one wanted to admit an entire family to the
psychiatric ward upstairs. The old man needed medical care; his Parkinsonian symptoms could be controlled, possibly relieved completely. All three were
badly undernourished, thin and rickety, pale and
gray. Anna's skin was a mess. Of the three the old
lady was the healthiest physically, and the craziest.
However, before they had been thrown out of their
apartment, they managed to escape the eyes of any
social agency, and functioned quite well outside of
an institution. Something obviously had to be done;
the sight of the family sitting hour after hour, day
after day, just sitting in that cold drab waiting room
waiting for someone to tell them what to do; the sight
of such complete abdication of self was beginning to

upset the staff. The decision was made to admit them temporarily to the psychiatric ward; to keep the old couple together in one room, and give Anna a room close by; and to ensure proper medical treatment for all three Gruners. The psychiatrists accepted this compromise unwillingly; they weren't interested in trying to work with an old lady who couldn't speak English, an old man jerking, rolling the minutes away, a middle-aged spinster quite awesome in her ugliness. Psychiatrically, they just weren't very interesting.

Everything was so accidental. If the landlord had not wanted to renovate the building, he wouldn't have pushed for eviction. If the marshal had served warrants on the Gruners so they could have known about the coming eviction, they might have tried to do something about it before that day. If the family hadn't been so frightened, they might not have fought the police, and would have just ended up walking the streets. But every step, every little incident, led them down the path to the state mental hospital; not so much because they were mad, or dangerous, or even unable to function. They just had no place else to go, and no strength to find a place, and were just weird enough for society to accept the burden of their support. They were poor, they were old, they were dirty, and they wouldn't cooperate. So, after a few weeks in the relative opulence of a city hospital receiving ward, the whole family was moved to a nearby state mental hospital. This time they were separated. Anna was sent to a regular ward, and her parents were sent to the geriatric section.

By this time I had come to know the family fairly well. Since they had been ripped from a home of thirty years, pulled rudely and brutally out of an environment they felt safe in, and all trace of their furniture and possessions had disappeared, they were increasingly disoriented. The old lady remained totally suspicious; finally one day, she pointed at me and said, "You Jewish?"

"No," I replied. That was the end of our conversations.

"She's not Jewish," the old lady would hiss whenever I came into the room. "Don't trust her, she's not Jewish." She was a thoroughly disagreeable old lady, full of petty suspicions, a tiny, boxed-in little mind, shrinking ever tighter inside herself. Nothing I could do could touch or move her; somehow, I was responsible for all their troubles, I was one of them, one of the enemy, a holder of the large keys that kept them locked in the hospital. "Don't trust her," the whisper would come with me into the room, filling the air with silent suspicion. And the old lady was right in some way; I was an agent, a part of the machine that was pulling, pushing, moving them around. I had the keys, she was a prisoner. I had some of the power to keep her locked up for the rest of her natural life.

Because of her suspicious and uncooperative behavior, the old lady succeeded in getting herself labeled psychotic. "Senile dementia, with paranoid ideas." Her behavior was certainly strange, She would come out of the room she shared with her husband, clutching a filthy paper bag containing all her personal things — a comb, a toothbrush, old tissues, some bright-colored yarn, her reading glasses, a piece of mirror — and, standing tightly up against the doorjamb, she would dart her eyes up, down, across the hall before moving an inch. And that is how she moved: inch by inch, shoulder tight up against the wall, eyes constantly moving, ready for danger and betrayal at every step. You could hear her slithering down the hall, sounding for all the world like an upright snake. And a few steps behind, slightly stumbling, a little unsteady, moved the old man.

Mr. Gruner was a little apologetic about everything. He seemed to say excuse me to the very air he breathed; to hesitate before each bite of food, as if he wasn't sure it was his to chew; to sit and walk in a way that made you understand perfectly the word "self-effacing."

He and his wife had come to the United States

sixty years ago, newly married and full of hope. They had paid their third-class passage with her wedding dowry. The village gathered silently to watch them leave; Mrs. Gruner cried all the way across, he told me.

"Now the village we were born in, the country of our birth, has disappeared. Yes, gone, the casualty of a revolution, a world war, geopolitics; now a whole people have lost their history. I find that sad in my old age. I remember my native dress, even my language. I close my eyes and try and imagine what has taken its place. Is there nothing? The emptiness causes a pain, a sadness of the spirit. A nation gone. This has something to do with why Sarah feels so confused now; so many things disappearing. She has no tears left. First her village gone, then her country. She never got accustomed to all the changes. Maybe if we hadn't left our village . . ."

And he would sit quietly for a few minutes, proud head bowed over his ruined body. In the hall I could hear Mrs. Gruner sliding down the wall, following her own path.

Mr. Gruner had been a printer, a typesetter, a skilled man before the Parkinson's disease became too debilitating. He had been a good union man, a fighter in the early days, and when he talked about those days when he had been trying to help organize the printer's union he seemed taller and more sure of himself. "Those were the days," he said, "the days when I was a man, when I took care of my family and fought the bosses at the same time. I was not a big man, but strong, strong in my heart. The union was the big thing, the important work of my life. Being a printer was a skill, a job for the hands; but the union was my heart. I was a workingman, yes, but a union man. That is important, those days. Even now it makes a difference. Typesetters make good money now, because me and mine went without food, without heat, to show the bosses we were stronger. We won so many fights, so many battles. But the war still goes on, you know, the war between big money and little workers. To work hard, always work hard, that is good and right for men and women; but you should have enough to live, to eat, to buy books. Only then you can call your soul and mind free. This old body of mine — look at it. Shaking away, getting better, maybe, but no good. The hands are no good anymore, and sometimes I can't even read. But when my check comes, my pension check that I get because I fought for a union, then I am a man again. It is not a gift, that money; neither is the other check, the social security check. I worked. My wife worked. Now we are old, and these are wages due us for a life of work, a good life."

"Don't trust her . . ." hissed Mrs. Gruner.

"We've had a hard time," continued the old man. His head, that beautiful strong head above the ruined body, was straight and proud as he talked about the past. "And my wife, she learned sometimes you can't trust anyone. One of her friends reported us to the police, and a goon squad broke up our home looking for union literature. And there were other times . . . in the old country . . . so excuse her. She gets a little confused, and doesn't understand you are trying to help, trying to find us a new home. Sometimes, even I can't remember why the police wrecked our home this time. I've been retired a long time; but maybe someone has a very long memory, and is trying to get us still. But they can't change things now. The union, the union is strong, now."

Mr. Gruner and I would have long conversations about the old days while Mrs. Gruner would act out her private fantasies around us. She would sometimes dart around the room, as if looking for a place to hide, and would stop suddenly, glance slyly in my direction, and move back to the wall. Most of the day she spent moving restlessly, endlessly, up and down the corridor. One day I noticed that her endless sliding, moving so close to the baseboard, was removing ten years' accumulation of dirt. You could see a little path, a place where some of the original pattern of the tile was showing through layers of old wax, old dirt, old soap. That was on "her" side of the corridor; the other side remained as dark and filthy as before. I pointed this out to one of the attendants one after·noon, saying that Mrs. Gruner was really cleaning the corners for them. As we stood in the hall laughing at the power of mad feet, Mrs. Gruner came sliding down the hall in our direction. The aide went over and took the old lady by the arm, laughingly urging her to clean the other side of the corridor. "Come on, honey, walk down *this* side for a bit. Come on, don't be so stubborn, move down this side." A desperate pulling match began; Mrs. Gruner was plainly terrified to leave "her" side of the corridor, for whatever crazy reasons, and the aide was bigger, stronger, and very insistent. Mrs. Gruner began to scream, to wail a high keening note, and spat in the attendant's face. The aide released the old lady, shoving her abruptly against the wall. Another aide came down the hall, and the two of them locked the old lady in a seclusion room for the rest of the day. "Patient became violent," read the report.

The ward staff began to talk about giving Mrs. Gruner shock treatments and separating her from her husband to prevent any deterioration in his condition. The doctor was moderate and very scientific; he said that shock treatments are particularly effective in cases of senile depression or when patients are violent. The social worker said it was important to maintain the family unit, but that the behavior of one must not be allowed to influence the other members, and that Mrs. Gruner was frequently upsetting to everyone. The attendants reported that Mrs. Gruner was uncooperative and suspicious, sometimes refusing to make her bed or bathe herself according to schedule. The recreation worker said that Mrs. Gruner did not participate in any ward activities. Everyone seemed to agree that the disagreeable old lady should have a hundred and thirty volts of electricity sent through her brain for three tenths of a second. Since all three members of the family were formally committed to a mental hospital, no approval from anyone else was necessary.

ECT. Electro-convulsive-therapy. I didn't even know they used it any more; I thought that since the so-called tranquilizing drugs were developed, shock treatment had largely been discontinued. In fact, at this particular hospital, no area was set aside for ECT and recovery rooms. But it seemed that patients could be sent down the street to the city hospital where facilities were available — and used.

The patient is sedated, wheeled into a room, the sticky jelly applied to both temples, and cold electrodes, running on wires from a little black box, are applied over the jelly. There is no noise, maybe just a little zzss! and the patient goes into a severe convulsion. Throws a fit. Muscles strain against the straps, jerking, pulling, twitching; a hollow gasping moan comes from the rubber tube placed in the mouth of the patient, and in a few seconds it is all over.

Except little bits and pieces of memory are wiped out. The patients are subdued, confused, disoriented for days after ECT. Yes, sometimes depressed people become less depressed, and violent people become less violent. You could say it is effective and, if judged by simple empirical standards, therapeutic. But I am prejudiced; it has always seemed to me that shock therapy is a violent, evil act in itself; when I was in nurse's training, I refused to hold the electrodes against the temple of the patients, refused finally to even watch, because it seemed to me the treatment was so much worse than the disease. The eyes of people who have had shock treatment always seem pained and a little vague. They spend a good deal of time trying to fill in the holes left by the hundred and thirty volts; the mind doesn't like to miss bits of history. Mrs. Gruner had suffered enough rude shocks lately — the loss of her home, the long confused days in the hospital waiting room, the move to the state hospital — and certainly had reason enough to act a little weird, even to act very weird. After all, she was eighty years old and had a right to some aberrant behavior. So I argued against ECT.

"Sentiment wins," said the doctor. "We'll let you try and straighten her out without shock. But her behavior must improve within a week or . . ." and he waved a languid arm in the general direction of something.

I left the meeting considerably shaken; Mrs Gruner was not going to respond to any magic therapy of mine within a week. All I had done was buy a little time. And protect my own conscience by taking a principled stand I knew would be overruled any moment. I stood in the corridor and looked at Mrs. Gruner's little path. Now what, for God's sake? Her brother would not accept any responsibility; Anna was just beginning to pull herself together, and was looking for a part-time job and a place to live; and Mr. Gruner was still in no physical shape to be moved out of the hospital.

The state mental hospital. Not too many old people end up there. Those wards are really the end of the road. The geriatric section is always the most unattractive, poorly lighted, no brightness, no pictures, no laughter. Just long green corridors, lined by doors; white-gowned nurses moving silently, expressionless;

large wards with beds filling the room, allowing no space for anything. Two things impress you: the silence and the smell of urine.

The door of the elevator would open quietly and the smell would tell you it was the geriatric section. When you stepped off, you found yourself trying to wall very quietly, as if not to wake a sleeping child. There were people there, you could feel them, but not a sound . . . then a door would open, you heard the heavy keys clanking at the belt of an attendant, and you knew there was life. I visited the Gruners infrequently; the old lady still did not trust me, but she always remembered me. I would try and bring the old man a copy of the Jewish newspaper, and he would smile sweetly, move his head in a courtly Old World manner, and ask me to sit down.

"Tell me," he said one day. "What is this shock treatment they want to do? Is it a good thing? Is my wife, then, being treated by old-fashioned methods? She is difficult, and old, and not easy to understand; but she does no harm."

They were so helpless. And so was I. I could no more stop the doctors from doing whatever they pleased to the old couple than they could. Once inside, once clamped in the public jaws of the mental hospital, the doctor knows best, knows all, makes all the decisions. Even if you are clever, and not too mad, you can't escape the force of decisions made by a man who may or may not have real interest in your case. Doctors who choose to practice in a state institution are not always imaginative and open-minded in their approach to problems. And Mrs. Gruner was a problem. I thought wildly of telling Mr. Gruner to gather his things together, take his wife by the hand and escape . . . where? He was looking at me, blue eyes a little watery with concentration, waiting for an answer.

"I think shock treatment is not a good thing. But your wife . . . if you could get her to be a little more polite to the attendants, participate more . . . she's such a cranky old lady . . . can you do anything with her?"

"My dear. No one has been able to change Sarah's ways for years; she has just been getting worse. I think that is what growing old is all about: whatever you are, it just gets worse. Like me, my shaking; fifty years ago no shaking, forty years ago a little tremor, thirty years ago I shake like a mild chill, and today — a regular earthquake, my body. The medicine helps me, but pills won't make Sarah an easy woman. Maybe for her the shock treatment will give a little rest from her meanness." His eyes were so blue, so kind; he was reassuring me, trying to say accept, accept, we can't change it by ourselves. "It isn't so bad here. And Anna is beginning to free herself. She, too, will never be a happy woman, but she should not be here. Here is for the old, and others who care nothing for their surroundings, such drab colors, such taste- less food. This is for the old and the mad. Not for Anna. She is not much to look at, but she can still find some satisfaction. In books, or movies, or a little dog, maybe. She should not be here. You get her out. Let the old care for the old; and you stop worrying."

My eyes were on the little path left by Mrs. Gruner around the edge of the floor. If they gave her shock treatment, could she move to the other side of the corridor? Would she learn to play musical chairs, or bingo, or whatever childish games were offered? I didn't think so; I thought they might slow her down for a little bit, but unless they were willing to burn out her mind, burn out all the stubbornness, all the meanness, all the secret parts of her head, she would remain a very, very difficult old lady. That was what Mr. Gruner was trying to say. I had to trust her as he did.

"Mr. Gruner, I'm sorry. I really don't think you be- long here, but I don't know how to get you out."

"I know, I know. There is a story about a room that only has a way in, no way out. You enter that room, and it is not a pleasant room, but you can't leave. The only way out, the characters find, is by death. That is what this place is to me. I know. I hope the wait is not too long; some of those people, vegetables lying in their own dirt, some of them have been here since this hospital opened. They are fed, cleaned, turned. They are not alive. And it is not easy for the staff to take care of them — look at their faces. The living pinched and hardened by caring for the dying. You must not get angry at them, they do a very hard job."

He was correct, of course. I did get very angry at the staff; at their coldness, their harshness, their sloppiness. They cared nothing for their patients. I don't know why they even did their job, except, maybe because someone like Mr. Gruner comes along, someone to talk to, someone who tries to understand. His careful courtesy and manner made him the darling of the ward, just as her crabbiness made his wife the pest. His clothing was always clean, and picked carefully from the piles of donated things sent to the ward. Special little things had a way of appearing on his tray at dinner. They fussed about his hair, which was really beautiful, thick and gray, brushed into high waves above his forehead. But his wife continued to wear almost the same clothes; I'm sure they were changed sometimes, but on her they always looked the same. She still hissed suspiciously at everyone and looked madly around corners. Nothing suited her.

191

I stopped seeing the Gruners when Anna left the hospital. For one thing, she wasn't there to make me feel guilty with her pitted face. For another, the trips upstairs were getting too depressing. The feeling of death and decay and madness was in every corner of the hospital, but on the geriatric wards you could taste it. I could not keep going up that elevator to talk to a ruined old man who had totally accepted his fate. Nothing could touch him; he had made his peace a long time ago. But I had not, and did not think I could tolerate seeing so much of the dirty inner workings of the society, the last place they reserve for the old, the senile, the mad, the dying. There was no room for dignity in that place, no space for a good place to die.

Twelve

PEOPLE who manage to survive to old age know that the present system is destroying them. They experience discrimination, intolerance and isolation based on the sole fact that they are old. Their oppression stems from an irreversible biological condition, as surely as a black person faces oppression because of color and a woman experiences oppression based on sex.

If you are over forty, you are unlikely to be promoted or, if unemployed, find a job. If you are sixty-five, you are forced to retire. If your hair grays, you must dye it. If your physical condition deteriorates — as it must — you will enter an institution. If you look for an apartment, people may refuse to rent to you; old people smell and can't take care of themselves. If you stop to watch children playing, you're suspected of being a dirty old pervert. There are a million derogatory names for you: "old biddy," "crazy old coot," "dirty old man," "silly old codger." If someone wishes to pay you tribute, they say you're so *young* — considering your age. That is as grievous an insult as telling a woman she "thinks like a man."

Traditional roles for the aged have vanished. There are no quiet, warm spaces by the fireplace to sit and watch your grandchildren play; no cracker barrels to sit upon and speak of times past. There is no security in old age.

It is not with respect that youth views age; youth grants the old neither greater wisdom nor greater prowess. The old are forced to walk slowly, fearfully, and alone. The young eye their bent bodies with disgust, fearful of the day when they, too, will walk with death. Between the young and the old is the uncertainty of middle age, where people cling frantically to signs of vanishing youth with hair dye, makeup, fancy exercises, fad diets, and clothing designed to ·camouflage the attack of time on their bodies.

Shame and suspicion are generated within our culture: The old are allowed to be quaint, eccentric, even angry. But they must remain silent, always the outsider. This is a culturally sanctioned attitude, caused by the fear of those caught in the middle of the three-tiered society; those who must pay the bills, the middle-aged, working American. Goaded by fear of their own aging, angry at the financial drain caused by the dependent young and the dependent old, jealous of youth and hating the dreary future, they exist in a world of nameless dread and uncertainty. They feel as if they work for everyone's happiness but their own. But there is no need to convince them of the oppression of old age; they will discover it soon enough.

I know we carry the burdens of the youth cultist well into old age; I know this makes many old people hate themselves, causes young people to avoid contact with the aged as they would exposure to smallpox, and is resulting in a strange sort of segregation of the old. I have learned that a culture which equates material possessions with success, and views the frantic, compulsive consumer as the perfect citizen, can afford little space for the aged human being. They are past competing, they are out of the game. We live in a culture which endorses what has been called "human obsolescence." After adolescence, obsolescence. To the junk heap, the nursing home, the retirement village, the "Last Resort."

I don't believe there ever truly existed a golden age for the so-called golden years. Even in the most traditional, ancestor-worshipping societies, I am sure families sometimes resented the responsibility of caring for their aged. The Chinese proverb "The old are the precious gem in the center of the household" probably caused not a few families to wonder why they had been stuck with a flawed stone. And nomadic tribes, such as the Eskimos and the Pygmies, left behind to die anyone who could not move with the tribe. I've seen families in the United States where grandparents were carefully provided for, in the bosom of the family, yet acts of kindness were frequently accompanied by martyred sighs.

There is an old American folk tale about a wooden bowl. It seems that Grandmother, with her trembling hands, was guilty of occasionally breaking a dish. Her daughter angrily gave her a wooden bowl, and told her that she must eat out of it from now on. The young granddaughter, observing this, asked her mother why Grandmother must eat from a wooden bowl when the rest of the family was given china plates. "Because she is old!" answered her mother.

The child thought for a moment and then told her mother, "You must save the wooden bowl when Grandma dies." Her mother asked why, and the child replied, "For when you are old."

There are a few obvious social changes that contribute to the increasingly sorry position of the aged in our society. The first is the changing structure of the nuclear family, second is the continuing revolution in work, and third is the development of the social welfare state. All three are interconnected and mutually supportive.

I have mentioned the decline of the extended family; that is, many generations existing in a more or less harmonious state under one roof. In the United States an affluent economy and advancement in medical care resulted in two things: earlier marriages for the young and longer lives for the old. This means that a person of forty may be a parent, a grandparent, *and* have living parents and grandparents.

As the family has become larger, with more generations to gap, the extreme mobility of our society means that each member probably lives in a different section of the country. There may exist no real closeness, no deep communication between members. When they get together it is likely to be an "occasion," more like a convention than a family gathering.

Or they may only see one another, write one another, in times of trouble. ("Johnny, your Great-aunt Sadie is dead." "Who?")

In any case, although the family is certainly quantitatively extending, the quality of relationships within the family is deteriorating. Love, respect, mutual responsibility — which are the only relevant bases for any human grouping — are no longer an integral part of the family. Each individual seems to stand alone, and is likely to regard family ties as an intolerable burden. The "family" has become just another institution, faintly archaic, unable to satisfy the emotional, psychological, and physical needs of its members.

Now we must deal with the notion that, in the United States, what a person does is what a person is. We are defined by our work. This myth has survived the technological advances which have rendered many jobs useless and unrewarding. The day of the skilled craftsman whose pride in his product gave satisfaction and prestige has passed. We have fewer and fewer people involved in production and more working in so-called service industries. We also have a conflict between medicine, which allows people to work to an advanced age, and the economic fact that the actual labor force is being diminished. While labor once fought for pension and retirement plans as a way of reducing the burden on people who could no longer stand to work, these benefits are now seen as a way to encourage early retirement and ensure jobs for younger workers.

You can see what this means for the older worker: While he is still feeling healthy and able, and believes that his job defines who he is, he must face both early retirement and the knowledge that his skills are obsolete. Moreover, if his life has been almost entirely centered around his work, that is, if he made most of his friends on the job, pursued hobbies related to the work, spent a good deal of his time talking about his work, the void left by the disappearance of that center can be devastating. There is no continuity of activities, relationships, interests; no stable long-term interests to fill the hours. The accepted American equation of job equals the person, means, in the last analysis, no job, no person.

Nobody knows or can predict the exact moment when a person realizes he is old; he may get the message from his body or from his family or from the sudden appearance of Boy Scouts to help him across the street. I would like to suggest that one of the most aging experiences an old man or woman can have is the first encounter with the social welfare state.

I am using the term "social welfare" in a very loose

sense; I mean agencies and institutions and organizations that employ people called "social workers" who have some measure of control over other people's daily lives. They are people who can give or withhold money; find a place to live for someone who is old or cause them to be sent to an institution; judge whether or not a person is fit or sane or able enough to live alone; organize "suitable" activities for the aged; run community centers; all of these and more. They possess a very real power of life and death among the aged in the United States. And they are usually motivated by goodwill toward men, equipped with little notebooks to note those worthy of goodwill, and promises to help if they can.

One old man I know calls them "little tin gods." Yet even as he speaks with scorn he is frightened. He is dependent on the goodwill of "his" caseworker and he knows it. I met the woman one day; she was young and hesitant and full of questions. Did his son send him money this week? Is the old man working at any extra job? Has he found a new place to live, that old hotel is filthy, full of cockroaches and drunks. What has he been eating. And on and on. She was about twenty-five, he was seventy-four and he was embarrassed for me to hear his obsequious replies to the young lady. Yes, ma'am, no, ma'am. And all the time worrying about whether or not he would receive his check from the New York Bureau of Social Services to supplement his meager social security allowance. The more anxious he got, the more questions the social worker asked. I could see her wondering, what has him so uptight? What is he trying to hide?

It was her job to be suspicious, and his job to tell as little as possible without losing his check. She must fill out a little form, judging, evaluating, deciding, observing; collecting data to allow him a little more to live on, while he must try and preserve a little privacy and self-respect.

The idea of "social welfare" seems so impersonal and rational from the outside. But when you see it in action and talk to the victims, human beings reduced to a little card, a few questions, found needy or not needy, found fit or unfit, found honest or dishonest, found clean or unclean; when you see the machine in action you want to spit in the eye of the earnest, well-meaning young lady. In the process of "helping" she, all unknowing blind goodwill, with four years of good liberal education and Christian sympathy, could so confuse and rattle that old man and feel only vaguely uncomfortable. After all, she was only trying to help.

Another example comes to mind: There are so many old people living alone in the city, without friends or family. One social worker I know decided to try and find a suitable apartment for several old people and encourage them to help one another. I thought it was a great idea, and the noble experiment was launched. A three-bedroom apartment in a fairly safe neighborhood was rented, and six old people — four women and two men — moved in. Communal living among the ancients! After the first few weeks of minor conflicts — usually about what they would eat, who washed the dishes last, and the usual problems found in any family — the group seemed quite stable and happy. The social worker hovered about with understandable pride. Everything was lovely. The group was a bit stiff and formal when visited, but obviously proud of the new living arrangements. They had regular meetings with the social worker, and to my amusement, seemed to present her with a weekly problem only she could solve. Mr. Jones was eating food meant for regular meals. Mrs. Smith persisted in cooking fried foods some of them could not digest. Mrs. Goldberg wanted linen changed more often. Small things, not very real, but they helped the social worker feel she was still part of this new "family," fruit not of her womb yet just as dear to her heart.

Then one day, in the course of a regular checkup, Mrs. Smith was found to have a large lump in her breast. Surgery was performed, the breast removed.

The growth was cancer and the doctor felt it had spread throughout her system. Further masses were found in her abdomen. She was dying.

This was a real problem, a crisis for a family not quite a year old. Mrs. Smith went home, knowing she was dying, to a worried family. She was pampered, fed special things, read to, cared for. At first, she was able to get around quite well; but becoming steadily weaker, spent more time in bed. The social worker was very concerned about the effect all this would have on the family. The group wanted Mrs. Smith to stay with them. They felt they could care for her. But the social worker decided to have Mrs. Smith sent to a nursing home.

That is real power. When I voiced an objection, I was told that it wasn't good for old people to have to dwell on thoughts of death. "Poor things," the social worker told me. "They have enough problems, just trying to survive, without having to face the fact of death right in their own home." She was adamant. It was her family, she had created it, and she would make decisions for their welfare. She knew what was best.

Mrs. Smith died in a nursing home, alone. Back in the apartment, the family was no longer a family. They were just a group of people living together on welfare, with a lady coming in to make decisions for them. It wasn't much of a home anymore. The last time I visited the apartment, it felt like any old hotel or boardinghouse. A collection of African violets which had been blooming wildly was dying; nobody cared for them. They had not been allowed to care for one of their own, had been cheated of assuming responsibility for each other, had even been robbed of the right to grieve.

I know that social worker meant well. She was a good-hearted woman, not evil in the least, yet I would never forgive her for hurting those old people. She abused them, used her power to degrade them, said they had no right to care for one another. I know she didn't mean to do that; in fact when I tried to talk to her about it, she couldn't understand what I meant. To her they were "poor old things" who must be carefully watched. After all, they hadn't been able to survive without her services, had they?

I have mentioned that to be old and poor is a full-time job. The number of workers required to help the aged wade through the bureaucratic tangle, and the multiple agencies available, just to get help, almost equals the aged population itself. In fact, there are so many agencies that another agency was formed in New York City to refer old people to the proper agency. It would be funny, but when you are old and haven't much energy to spare, "going the rounds" to get "benefits" and "assistance" and "counseling" would seem to be a process guaranteed to lead to an early grave.

And that is only one aspect of the problem. The lack of understanding shown by intelligent people toward their clients is the saddest sight of all. Damn it, I know the social workers mean well. I don't think they would take such jobs if they didn't care. But something happens to them when they face another human being across that chasm dividing the worker from the poor. Maybe the social worker just sees too much human misery and becomes callous. Maybe they have to learn to shut off their emotions in order to do the job. Maybe their case load is too heavy for them to spare any human interest in their clients, for time is so short and the aged poor so numerous.

But I think the failure is built right into the social welfare system. We are a nation built on the principle of rugged individualism. We believe in a fair day's pay for a fair day's labor. We give value for value received. Yet here is an entire bureaucracy, a huge complicated system encompassing all levels of government plus various private and religious groups, founded on the principle that some people cannot take care of themselves and must receive charity. The system is constructed in such a way to separate, forever, the givers from those who must receive. Lack of understanding — of empathy — on the part of those who work within the system, and shame on the part of those who ask for help makes communication impossible. Both sides become angry, resentful, scornful. People do not like to be cast in the role of victim or victimizer. They react badly. They cease to regard one another as human.

Furthermore, it is a terribly inefficient system. Both sides complain about the amount of paperwork necessary, of the duplication of effort, of the time lost and the arbitrary rules. It obviously must be changed, stripped of pettifoggery and obfuscation and that aura of total power. Why should an old person be shamed, on top of all the other burdens, simply because he must seek a bed, a meal, clothing?

Critical analysis of an oppressive situation is always too easy. I began this book with a few ideas, a few stories to tell that I thought would illuminate the problems. I wanted to share my thoughts about our North American culture and its relationship to our attitudes about aging. I spent many hours, over a period of two years, with old people in the different areas of the United States, and tried to listen carefully, observe closely, and learn just what it means to be old in America.

This approach leaves me in the position of an outsider. I tried to live with the old and the problems they face but the fact remains I am not old — yet. I can see a time in my future when I must face old age and dying, but that is a long way off. I do find our cultural resentment of the process of aging unnatural. I look in the mirror and am sometimes shocked, sometimes amused, sometimes saddened by the changes I see taking place day by day, little by little. The bones in my face are becoming more prominent, lines are forming about my mouth and my eyes, my long nose looks even longer. When I am very old I will probably look like a Halloween witch. The skin on my body is a little less taut, a little less flexible this year than last; my thighs seem a bit crepey and my ankles swell. I'm getting more freckles. I do regular exercises to stay fit, to be able to wear that bikini one more year. Like a racehorse trained too young and ridden too hard, I sometimes feel as if my wind and stamina have been expended too far in advance. The body seems to collect on all those old debts, requiring that I rest more frequently and exercise less strenuously. Being with old people has helped me understand these changes in my body. If I tend to emphasize the importance of physical changes in determining adjustment to old age, it is because I am beginning to feel those changes strongly.

One thing that I am trying to suggest is that physical aging is a process we are all going through. Our response to this natural process has been twofold: sentimental nonsense and deliberate ignorance. Instead of listening to our bodies, obtaining all the knowledge we can, and adjusting life-styles accordingly, we produce enormous anxiety among the aged if they cannot maintain the same level of activity and the same unlined face as someone who is thirty. Or, instead of expecting far too much, we assume that anyone over fifty or so has one foot in the grave and is fit only for the rocking chair. Why shouldn't we strive to develop a nonjudgmental acceptance of the changes that come with age?

If we could change the picture we have of old people and view life as more of a continuous circle, with different paces suitable to different ages, perhaps we could learn to view old people as human beings with a future as well as a past. Instead of seeing a picture of himself as a doddering old fool, which is the reflection an old person is apt to see in society's mirror, the elderly could begin to feel more vital and become less of a "burden" and more a part of whatever community they chose to live among. There are many ways to contribute to society, and most of them do not require youth. We have learned to act as if that were true, choosing to emphasize the negative qualities of the aged.

It is quite true that with age comes a need for reassurance, anxiety about being abandoned, fear of isolation. But these are not qualities of aging itself; they are feelings generated by the lack of respect the aged face every day. There is a curious contradiction here: We no longer view someone who is sixty as incredibly old, yet we think that a proper age to put people out to pasture.

Even allowing for the mental and physical slowdown accompanying old age, there are many jobs and activities old people are capable of performing. I don't mean the nonsense make-work projects which are so eagerly dreamed up by the directors of senior citizen centers but real ways the aged could continue to contribute to society. Nothing is so depressing as seeing a roomful of people engaged in performing some task for no reason other than to fill empty hours. Painting pretty pictures is fine — if that is what you want to do. Playing bingo can be fun; knitting is productive and good for arthritic fingers; square dancing is joyful besides being good exercise. But what if those were the only alternatives offered to, say, a twenty-five-year-old Rhodes scholar? Wouldn't you say it was a disgraceful waste? And don't you think the young person in question would suffer from a severe loss of self-respect if he could not use the knowledge and talent he possessed? He would probably become moody, withdrawn, hostile, and suicidal. Yet such is the position of many of our aged. And they, too, become moody, withdrawn, and suicidal.

I realize there is already a severe unemployment problem in the United States, and increasing pressure on businesses and labor unions to encourage early retirement in order to create more jobs for the young. Yet in a society that emphasizes competence, hard work, and productivity, it is degrading to suddenly become nothing more than a passive consumer, sitting with idle hands while still in possession of the physical and mental ability to do a job.

Nobody but the aged themselves can solve this problem. Social workers, doctors, organizers, the clergy — all are believers in the myth that old age means total retirement. I know people enter retirement unprepared for what all those golden leisure hours will bring, in spite of the fact that many large companies now have mandatory lectures for people who are about to retire. Maybe the problem is with the word "leisure." That isn't something you do fulltime, no matter what your age.

The father of one of my friends recently retired after thirty years as a successful furniture salesman. He is a quiet, gray little man, but filled with one ambition. He had always wanted to be a carpenter. Dur-

ing his youth and middle age he had been unable to
pursue this ambition; partly, I suspect, because of the
low status associated with such a vocation in the eyes
of his wife. Now he felt free to learn a trade, if only
as a part-time job. He knew several people in the
building professions and went to them with his plan:
Take me on as an unpaid apprentice, teach me to
build things, and then, if I have any ability, hire me
on little jobs. Or, once I learn how to handle the
tools, maybe I can do free-lance carpentry — be a
handyman.

Everyone turned down his offer. One man said the
unions would object, even if he wasn't on the payroll,
because he would be competing for jobs needed for
younger men. Another said that his insurance
wouldn't cover an old man. Another just refused to
take him seriously, slapped him on the back, and told
him to buy golf clubs and learn how to play.

So he finally went to a local trade school and tried
to enroll in their carpentry class. He was refused admission, again on the grounds that he was too old,
and told to try one of the local senior citizen centers
which had a hobby shop. The center did, in fact,
have classes advertised as "Instruction in Woodworking." But these classes concentrated on learning how
to burn uplifting messages into carefully shaped
pieces of wood and building pipe racks. The sort of

thing known as arts and crafts. This was not what he was interested in.

Mr. Hawk went back to the small apartment he shared with his wife, and suggested to her that he turn a seldom used guest room into a workshop. She refused, citing noise, dirt, expense, and the general craziness of his obsession. Other men are content to relax, she said. Why don't you? Now he does nothing, doesn't even dream anymore.

That is the nature of the opposition. It is as if the whole edifice of Western civilization rose up to destroy one man's dream. And if old people try, and try seriously, to remain productive members of the community, there will be many who will call them fools, others who will refuse to take them seriously, and worst of all, people who will try to show them the way and take over the whole enterprise. Every time a group of oppressed people rises up and tries to change their situation, someone gets anxious. I am reminded of a project in which residents of an old people's home began to take an interest in the residents of a home for the mentally retarded located nearby. Great idea, for who is better qualified to spare a little patience and give a little love than a lonely old person? Everything went smoothly, just informal visits, quiet reading hours, old voices raised in barely remembered lullabies.

The tragedy was that it was too good to be left alone. Someone decided it had to be organized, formalized, structured, observed, and supervised by responsible authorities. Classes were instituted to teach the old people how to handle retarded children. Printed schedules for visits and what would take place on those visits began to appear. The showing of too much physical affection was discouraged, and it was implied that there was something faintly, well, you know, *perverted* about the whole enterprise.

I don't really know the end of the story; the woman who told me about it just said she soon lost interest. It was true, she told me, that she had a favorite among the children and spent most of her time with her. "But they made me feel guilty about loving that child, as if an old fool like me and a young fool like her couldn't have any need to love and be loved. They said we had to do things just so, and that took all the love out . . . Maybe they were right. I couldn't be around to care for that child forever, but I didn't think it would actually harm her to have a little affection. They made me feel that I'd done something wrong."

Anyone with any experience with institutions could have told that old lady what she did wrong. She stepped outside of total dependence on the institution, and took the child with her. The integrity and power of the institution, as felt by its staff, was threatened. So the Kafkaesque "they" resumed control, and in the process, destroyed something quite beautiful. Even if the project, in some modified form, continues, the relationship between the old people and the retarded children will remain part of the total institution, less human, less spontaneous and less enjoyable. Instead of the old people doing something they want to do, and taking pride in that act, they will feel exploited, used as unpaid labor.

I wish that the old people in that home had not let themselves be defeated; but I suspect they didn't know until too late that the battle was on. And if you think about what life in most of those institutions we have built for our aged is like, maybe they were beaten before they started. The old are supposed to be a burden, not a resource.

According to a recent news story, more and more of us are getting older and older. The time of the youth cult is passing, and the balance of population is tilting in the other direction. I would like to suggest the obvious fact that people of all ages have a vested interest in changing the oppressive system I have tried to describe.

My family is very large; large enough, in fact, that I will never have to face the problem of what to do with the old folks. Also, both sides seem to have the ability to die with their boots on, that is, stay hale and hearty to a very advanced age. But I know that millions of Americans face the problem of what to do with Crazy Aunt Jane or an aged relative who simply cannot be cared for at home. I wish I could offer some hope, some alternative for these families. But there are no Utopian communities available for the senile, the debilitated, the bedridden. I know many families continue to care for their own, at tremendous prices to themselves.

I think some sacrifices are too great. For all the good intentions of the family, for all the worry about doing the right thing, sometimes it becomes necessary to face the fact that the aged person, however loved and cherished, must enter some sort of institution. When that decision is reached it should be made with the full knowledge that the facilities available, although some are better than others, are still institutions. They are not homelike, they are depressing, they are almost always understaffed, and nobody likes them. But it is sometimes an unavoidable reality. So far, in this society, we have not discovered how to make *any* institution fit for human occupancy; and most especially have we failed to create institutions for those who can no longer exercise any measure of control over their own lives. It is not even solely an economic problem; the more expensive places smell better, are decorated more tastefully, and have better-trained staff. But the atmosphere is the same. So if you do have to make such a decision, be as selective as you can, trust your own judgment, and don't blame yourself. Then sit down and think about how it could have been different, what could be changed, what you can do to lessen your guilt. Then do it.

I admit I cannot get too excited about reform measures; whenever one tries to change things within the existing structure, it always seems to me that the basic evils remain the same. There are some organizations which are trying to better the condition, if not the status, of old people.

There is the National Council on Aging, formed to encourage research into the problems of the aged, and serving as a sort of general clearing house of information. For example, they compile a directory of facilities available to the aged, listing requirements for admission, prices, and so on. They also provide data for legislators pertinent to the problems of the old.

The two largest membership organizations of the elderly are The American Association of Retired Persons and its affiliate, The National Retired Teachers Association. For two dollars a year, members receive a bimonthly publication called *Modern Maturity*. This is full of news about legislation affecting the old, stories about special projects for the aged, some advice and uplifting messages, and reports on conventions. The publication is not very interesting in itself, but the combined membership of AARP and NRTA is between three and four million. The magazine has plenty of advertisements for products geared to its readership. I am not too sure what the actual benefits of being a member of one of these organizations can be; they do offer special insurance coverage, special package trips "with your peers" and fun-filled conventions, often addressed by no less a personage than the President of the United States. As an organization, they also operate as a pressure group to encourage the passage of legislation benefiting the aged.

In this respect, there are many organizations operating in the same field. The aged form a very large bloc of voters — twenty million people, most of whom *do* vote — and, at least during election years, politicians address themselves to the aged. There is a prestigious Senate Committee on Aging which holds frequent hearings into the special problems of the old. But I wonder what all this activity really amounts to? I wonder what real difference it makes that seventeen specialists in the field of gerontology appeared before a senate committee and said . . .

what did they say? Nothing new. They just keep saying over and over, "Ain't it awful." And government, having thus shown their interest in twenty million people, can relax a bit, vote for a little increase in social security payments, tell the Food and Drug Administration to look into the latest quackery fad and the newest type of fraud, get their names in the paper and, I'm afraid, forget it. I say that because I see nothing new coming from the politicians, just the same old bone thrown over and over again. It is apparent to me that the heads of those organizations formed to protect the interests of old people, and the politicians who solemnly express sincere concern about the aged, and the special interest groups such as the owners of nursing homes, and the eminent gerontologist-sociologist-psychologist, all suffer from the same blindness and poverty of imagination. They would reduce all the problems of old age into one little package that could be solved with more money. Sometimes I almost believe it myself.

But it is not just a question of money. Look at the old man, the millionaire, sitting in his mansion, terrifying his family with threats of cutting them out of his will, using the power of his money to force some measure of respect, at least outwardly, from his family and the world. Do you think he is any less alien-

ated, any less frightened, any less full of self-hate
than the old woman who picks through a garbage
can? He has more power, that is true; if he is lucky,
his family won't try and have him declared incompe-
tent and senile and rob him even of that little bit. But
he is still a victim of our cultural attitude toward old
age. The people around him will assume they know
better what he needs than he does; his control over
little things like his diet will begin to slip; his favorite
niece will still refer to him as "poor old Uncle" and
pat his head in a condescending manner. He is oppressed because of his age and all the money in the
world won't change that.

The question now arises as to whether or not there
exists an alternative. After all, old age is biological
and you can't really change that. Someone did once
remark that if biology were destiny, then we would
have to change biology. And medical research is beginning to deal with some of the problems of aging,
making good health possible for longer periods of
time.

Let me say again that any real change will have to
originate with the old themselves. I think it is time
for old people to turn their energies toward discover-
ing their common oppression; to move from thinking

about safe, gracious living out in some planned community to a fight for self-respect and their right to a place in the larger community.

The first step in this revolution could be made by borrowing a technique from the women's movement. This would be to begin to form "consciousness raising groups," gatherings of old people where they can talk about what they think is wrong, where the roots of their misery lie, what makes them accept second-class citizenship. These groups are unled, uncontrolled by "professionals," and meant to raise passion and rile the blood, until the group, as a group, begins to feel a common bond and a common struggle.

The tactic of consciousness raising works. Women began forming small groups for the purpose of discussing common problems about six years ago. I remember those early meetings; at first we were shy and secretive, unable to speak about anything except the most public forms of our oppression. (For example, job discrimination.) But as we became more of a group, and learned to trust one another, we became more open. We began to speak of how we felt about being a woman, about our deepest shames and secrets, about our anger against being without power.

It is difficult to describe the joyousness of that early discovery: Finding out that other women had the same problems, learning ways to struggle together to free ourselves from the weight of self-hate and second-class citizenship gave us all new pride and new energy. A new feminist movement began from these small groups.

The word spread quickly and consciousness raising groups seemed to be forming everywhere, among conservative suburban housewives as well as young political activists. No one led this movement; it just grew, the techniques and theories spreading by word of mouth rather than through the media. Of course, the media discovered the movement soon enough, until today you find stories on the women's movement in every publication. And there has been plenty of criticism and resistance, some humorous and some merely vile. But women continue to struggle, continue to "raise their consciousness." Nobody laughs at the power of women anymore.

Old people can begin to get together in the same way. I can very easily imagine a group consisting of all the people whose stories I have told: the oppression of old age cuts across class lines, across differences in education and sex. The groups could study the strange lack of improvement in the status, the care and the understanding of the aged in this society. They could share their fears about death, about debilitating illness, about money. Any direction to their movement would rise organically from the new understanding and the new bonds formed in such groups. I can see them meeting in the lobbies of pensioner hotels, taking over senior citizen centers, gathering in the parks.

With the new consciousness, the old could "rise up angry." The programs and actions would be very flexible; everyone would pursue a direction according to interest and ability. But they would be united in one idea: To destroy the pathetic devices used to force old people out of society. They can plot and plan, agitate and investigate, use anything and everything so that the problem be recognized for what it is — oppression — and so that a *new* way for the aged is secured. The struggle will be arduous, long, and some old people will not live to see the end. But it can be done.

Recognition should be given to some of the opposition. There is a whole new group of "social workers" who have tried and failed to control other minorities, but seem to require "do-gooding" in the direction of someone they can feel superior to, and unthreatened by, in order to maintain their righteous self-confidence. They aren't going to like being told what to do by the people they are supposed to serve. They are going to find it difficult to deal with angry, proud demands rather than obsequious requests. And any movement among the old will receive the attention of the industries who profit from the sixty billion dollars a year old people spend on special products. The new science of gerontology, which up to now has had a wealth of passive subjects, may object to the demand that science turn toward the *felt* problems of aging.

Once old people stand up and say, "Stop feeling sorry for me!" lots of people are going to be left with nothing to say except, "What do you people want?" Watch out for that question; it is a trap. At first, I admit with shame, I thought all old people wanted was the right to die with dignity. But I was wrong. There are possibilities, alternatives, to the way old people live. Death can come at any age, and it is too final an answer.

Perhaps the newly conscious aged could investigate the possibility of a different type of extended family; more tribal, more flexible, more responsive, with less enforcement of roles according to age. There could be many age groups in this new social unit and alliances formed according to interests and inclination. The old could teach what they know as well as gain new skills. There would be exposure to more rather than less stimulation — ideas, sensuality, politics, action, life-styles — with horizons broadening in old age rather than becoming more limited.

They could stop the practice of forcing old people

into institutions "for their own good" by families, social agencies, and disability in two ways: first by removing the loss of self-respect which accompanies early retirement and the emotional starvation caused by the loss of any place in the community; and secondly, by developing ways to care for and support one another. In fact, maybe they could destroy the institutions altogether.

They could force society to accept the concept of a guaranteed income — regardless of age, prestige, or sex — which would be enough to take care of basic physical needs. This would be given without the interference of investigators and without stigma attached. People could pursue specialized interests for their own sakes, work if they wanted, and continue to contribute to society without the pressure of worry about money.

These are only a few ideas, limited by the fact that an individual imagination — mine — is making the suggestions. But imagine twenty million newly awakened, newly conscious old people, with their qualities of maturity and wisdom, no longer accepting oppression because they are old, getting together as a force for change. Their ideas would not only be unlimited, they would be illuminated by greater experience. A revolt of old people could change the entire structure of our society.

Once, after a rather spectacular automobile accident, I woke up in an emergency room staring into the eyes of a priest who was attempting to administer the Last Rites of the Catholic Church. "Jesus Christ, man, I'm not dead yet," I remember shouting. He retreated and I slipped into a coma which lasted a week. I would sometimes reach a semiconscious state during which I was aware that doctors, nurses, friends and family surrounded my bed and seemed to be waiting for me to die. I tried to tell them I wasn't finished, I wasn't ready to die, and the effort to communicate would make me slip back into a state where I felt very near death. It was as if I existed in two worlds, one full of color and pain and the other gray and empty. I was aware of my surroundings yet unable to communicate. Sometimes I felt so alone, so divorced from everything around me, entirely without desires or needs, that I thought I was dead.

Ever since that brush with the grave I have thought a good deal about dying. I remember during that time I resented very much the thought that I was going to die as the result of a stupid accident. I was ashamed of the manner of my dying, just another statistic lying in a hospital bed. It felt wrong to have my life end in such sudden oblivion. I believe that the emptiness I felt when faced with my own death was a result of the lack of meaning in my life. I had, literally, thrown my life away. I think I gained some wisdom from that experience as well as some spectacular injuries.

What did I learn? Well, I learned to be concerned with the entire quality of my life, to widen my world view to include more than just the passing moment. I learned that I was going to die, eventually, and that I had to live with the face of death peering at me in odd moments. I gained some sort of strength, maybe just a belief in my own integrity and my ability to experience anything, even death, with understanding.

I realize that we live in a culture which does not wish to concern itself with either death or aging. The old walk with death as a close companion yet find few people who will recognize that fact. I am trying to understand the relationship between the living and the dying, between old age and death. Why do some people face death with such quiet dignity, some people resist stubbornly, beyond human comprehension, refusing to die even when they are nothing but shells, without memory, without past, without future? Why are some lives like circles complete, full and smooth and a pleasure to look upon, while others seem like unpaved roads, unfinished visions, superficial patterns drawn in the sand?

As I spoke with old people, I became more and

more aware of the fact that our culture does not have a concept of the whole of life. Instead, life is divided into childhood, adulthood, and old age. Instead of a cycle, a vision of unity, we have a vision of stages, in which only one — adulthood — has the possibility of being lived productively, independently, and vigorously. Old age is viewed as a childlike state, but without the charm and promise. It is as if we wanted to finally view our lives as totally devoid of meaning, where the dependency and childishness of old age wipe out the accomplishments of adulthood. The experiences of a lifetime disappear in the feeling of being useless and passed by.

There is a pettiness in this vision of life. It totally ignores the fact that death is a part of life, that facing death is one of the noblest things about old age. Strength and dignity, maintained in the face of declining abilities, should be part of the total life experience. Avoiding looking at the entire life cycle, pretending that death doesn't exist, or is somehow in bad taste, robs the old of the chance to complete their life. It denies that death has any meaning, that there is any knowledge or experience to be gained in dying as well as in living, and leaves only a sense of despair.

That is the final robbery, the last indignity we impose on our aged Americans. They are not allowed to be conscious of the last experience, not permitted to view death as part of a completely integrated life. They must die in despair, feeling only that there is nothingness, they are nothing, death is nothing.

Somehow we have to change that. The anguish of a life without meaning, and a death without wisdom, should haunt us all. If the aged could "rise up angry" and refuse to be victims of either debilitating poverty or passive consumerism, and refuse to be treated as children, they will gain materially and spiritually. They could also pass on to the new generations a gift of life, an example of dignity in the face of death itself.